HOME PRESERVES

DATE DUE

PRINTED IN U.S.A.

Preservation Society

HOME PRESERVES

100 MODERN RECIPES

CAMILLA WYNNE

Robert ROSE

For complete cataloguing information, see page 192.

Disclaimer
The recipes in this book have been carefully tested by our kitchen and our tasters. To the best
of our knowledge, they are safe and nutritious for ordinary use and users. For those people
with food or other allergies, or who have special food requirements or health issues, please
read the suggested contents of each recipe carefully and determine whether or not they may
create a problem for you. All recipes are used at the risk of the consumer.

   We cannot be responsible for any hazards, loss or damage that may occur as a result of any
recipe use. For those with special needs, allergies, requirements or health problems, in the
event of any doubt, please contact your medical adviser prior to the use of any recipe.

Design and production: Kevin Cockburn/PageWave Graphics Inc.
Editor: Sue Sumeraj
Recipe editor: Jennifer MacKenzie
Proofreader: Kelly Jones
Indexer: Gillian Watts
Photography: Étienne Marquis
Food stylist: Camilla Wynne

Page layout adapted from *Les Conserves selon Camilla*, designed by Marc Rimmer.

The publisher gratefully acknowledges the financial support of our publishing program by the
Government of Canada through the Canada Book Fund.

Published by Robert Rose Inc.
120 Eglinton Avenue East, Suite 800, Toronto, Ontario, Canada M4P 1E2
Tel: (416) 322-6552 Fax: (416) 322-6936
www.robertrose.ca

Printed and bound in Canada

1 2 3 4 5 6 7 8 9 TCP 23 22 21 20 19 18 17 16 15

To my dearly departed grandmothers,
Molly MacLachlan and Gwenneth Ingr.
I wish you were here to see this.

CONTENTS

◦❧◦

INTRODUCTION

It may come as a surprise, but I never canned a single jam, jelly or pickle until I was in my early twenties. I grew up in Edmonton, Alberta. My mother never canned — we never had a vegetable garden, and she often worked two jobs, so there was never any need, nor the time. My father, while an excellent cook, didn't can either. Both of my grandmothers, on the other hand, were fantastic preservers. Granny Ingr, originally from Wales, would make the most delicious black currant jam using the berries from her urban backyard garden. Grandma MacLachlan, who lived on an amazing farm called Sunny Slopes, had a vast root cellar full of jars. My absolute favorite were her canned raspberries, probably covered in syrup and processed the same morning they were picked. However, neither grandmother ever taught me how to can. I'm not sure why I didn't insist. After all, canned fruits and pickles were great loves of my young life. I remember pining over store-bought cans of apricots in syrup, which my father didn't let me eat unless we had no fresh fruit at all in the house. As for pickles, I even drank the brine. I loved vinegar so much and consumed it so freely that I developed a sensitivity and couldn't have it at all for a few years of elementary school.

All that said, I've still never canned a thing in my native Alberta. As soon as I graduated from high school, I hightailed it to Montreal, Quebec, and have called it my home ever since. After a few years of university, I realized I was spending most of my time dreaming of cakes and planning what I would bake on the weekends. So I dropped out and enrolled in pastry school. It was during that time that I made my first batch of Seville orange marmalade (still my true love),

using a can of prepared oranges imported from England that I got at Gourmet Laurier. Such a funny idea to make canned goods using another can, but it hooked me. Soon after, I made my first marmalade from real citrus fruit, under the tutelage of Patrice Demers at Les Chèvres. I wrote down the recipe and made it for my whole family for Christmas.

That time was a golden age for me. I got hired by Les Chèvres and was lucky enough to work for many years with Patrice and, later on, his assistant Michelle Marek, a pastry chef who really fueled my love of canning. Michelle makes amazing preserves, and we would spend our off-hours making things like kumquat marmalade together. She had gone out to Berkeley and met June Taylor, a West Coast jam legend, and shared her discoveries with me.

By this point, I was starting to can enough that I almost had too much to give away. I might have started a preserves company right then, I suppose. Instead, I joined a band and spent the next five years making records and touring. As much as working in the world of fine dining opened my mind and my palate to amazing foods and techniques, touring played a part in my culinary education as well. There is no way I would have been able to visit almost every U.S. state and European country otherwise. And everywhere we went (often to the annoyance of my bandmates), I made it a priority to seek out foods I knew I might only get to try once. I won't ever forget the tiny fresh figs in Slovenia, the kolaches at a truck stop in Texas, the best macarons I've ever eaten in Tokyo, my first deep-fried pickles in New Orleans or, in Paris, taking a cab from the venue the second sound check had wrapped up and spending 80 euros at pastry shop Pain de Sucre. I loved playing music with that band, and I'm so lucky to have seen some of the world that way.

Inevitably, however, the band broke up (it was, after all, intentionally made up of weird strangers), and I found that, while I'd been traipsing around in a van playing songs, my contemporaries had become incredible pastry chefs. I was fortunate enough that two of my good friends employed me for a while, but I needed to do something on my own. I'd been canning a lot in the months spent at home between tours, and I'd even begun to sell some of my preserves on the side. It seemed to me that canning might also afford me a schedule I could play with, as opposed to the rigid, early hours of a pastry shop. To someone used to either working late shifts in restaurants or playing rock shows, that seemed very appealing.

So Preservation Society was born: a very personal, very particular preserves company. I may not always make pristine preserves from organic, heirloom produce, but I make things with heart. I love Montreal, and I love Quebec's focus on *produits du terroir* (literally "products of the territory" — our local foods), but let's face it, we're not in California, and there are only so many fruits we are able to grow here. My mandate at Preservation Society is to use as much local produce as possible, but I'm afraid that stops short at marmalade. The fruit I need to make my favorite preserve comes from very far away, and if I'm canning, I have to be making marmalade. Of course, if you are lucky enough to live somewhere citrus fruits are grown locally, more power to you! I'm jealous. Whenever I can, I use local produce, but in the dark winter months, imported citrus lights up my life.

As much as it seems like a nice idea to make the perfect strawberry jam, that's not really what I do, nor what you'll find in this book, for the most part. I like to amuse myself. That might just be the company philosophy. I like to take a boring ingredient — celery, for instance — and make it fun, as by pickling it in a Bloody Caesar–flavored brine. There's a reason I loved working in fancy restaurants, and why I did an internship at wd~50 in New York, where we made bath-bead-like spheres out of pomegranate juice. Molecular gastronomy can be playful; it references memories and places and other dishes; it transmogrifies ingredients in surprising ways. That experience made a big impression on me as a young pastry chef. So you won't find a recipe for straight-up strawberry jam here, I'm afraid, but you will find a jam inspired by the French Revolution.

I don't use very complicated techniques or, for the most part, hard-to-find ingredients, but I do like to mix classic recipes with some unique creations (more often than not, it seems, inspired by cocktails). And I hope to equip you to do the same. Sharing knowledge has always been part of the Preservation Society philosophy. Canning has its limits, to be sure — there are important rules to follow to ensure a safe product. But there are ways that you can safely put your own personal stamp on a recipe. After you get the hang of it, I hope this book serves as a launching pad for your own weird ideas.

PRESERVING BASICS

Having a pantry stocked with homemade canned goods is like having an arsenal of (benign) secret weapons. They act as instant gifts (hostess, birthday or otherwise), instant cocktail garnishes, instant snacks and food with a long shelf life that will nourish you in the event of a disaster. Canning allows you to control the ingredients that go into your prepared foods, can save you money (though if you're like me and are putting up kumquats in brandy and the like all the time, not really), and will preserve a glut of garden produce for the winter (if you're lucky enough to have a glut). There is really nothing like being able to eat your own apricot jam in the dead of February, or having a Concord grape spritzer on New Year's. Seasonal flavors that are fleeting can be captured like bugs in amber (though infinitely more palatable). Although you might be required to toil at the stove and chopping block for hours in the middle of the hottest summer, canning will ultimately bring the utmost joy into your life.

The most important thing to keep in mind when starting to can is that you need to make sure to follow the recipe you are using pretty strictly. Unfortunately, you can't just go ahead and can your favorite salsa or ratatouille recipe. The safety of your canned goods depends very much on their acidity, which is precisely calibrated for each recipe. Decreasing salt or acid could result in a risky product. But that's not to say there's no room for creativity — feel free to experiment with herbs, spices and other flavorings that will put a personal touch on your preserve. For instance, bread and butter pickles are all well and good, but substituting malt vinegar for white and adding garlic and ginger makes them exciting and British-tasting. Easy.

As far as safety is concerned, most things that can go wrong with canned goods will be pretty apparent if they do go wrong. If your preserve is discolored, has anything weird growing in it, smells bad or explodes, it's safe to say that you should sacrifice it to the garbage. Botulism, on the other hand, is totally undetectable and can cause terrible illness and even death. But if you follow current, published recipes from a reputable source and process your jars in a boiling water canner for the specified amount of time, all bacteria will be successfully annihilated. Botulism is also of little worry in jams and pickles, which are high-acid foods, as it thrives in a moist, airless, low-acid environment. At any rate, I have been canning like a madwoman for years now and have had just two bad jars — both of which were pretty obviously bad and also the result of neglecting the processing step. This final step is very important: boiling the filled jars in hot water for a specified amount of time ensures that the contents become hot enough all the way through to kill any potential bacteria.

If you own any canning books published in Europe, you may find that they have far laxer sterilization standards than North American guides. Many of our parents or grandparents also canned using methods that are now considered unsafe: sealing jars with paraffin wax, for instance, or covering canned tomatoes with a blanket instead of heat-processing them. As far as I know, no one ever got sick from my granny's preserves, but my feeling is, if we have the knowledge and the ability, why not follow a few extra steps to ensure that our canned goods won't spoil? I don't think we need to be scared to can — a lot of people in my classes wonder if they might perhaps kill someone by mistake — but it's a good idea to know the rules.

STERILE CANNING BASICS

1. Wash your jars in warm, soapy water and rinse them well, or wash them in a dishwasher, then submerge jars in a pot of hot water, bring the water to a simmer and keep the jars hot until it's time to fill them. Remove each jar and drain well just as you're ready to fill it.

2. Always use new snap lids and wash them in hot, soapy water before use. It has been common practice to heat the lids to soften the sealing compound before placing the lids on the jars. However, some manufacturers no longer require this to be done. I find it unnecessary, but you may still wish to do so. If you do, place the metal discs in a saucepan of hot (not boiling) water. Leave the pan off the heat and cover it to keep the lids warm while you fill the jars.

3. To protect the jars, place a metal rack or dish towel in the bottom of your largest pot, which you will use as your boiling water canner. Fill the pot with water, cover and heat until steam starts to escape. Reduce the heat to low and leave the pot until your filled jars are ready.

4. Once you have prepared your recipe, fill the jars, leaving the amount of headspace specified in the recipe —

generally $1/4$ inch (0.5 cm) for 8-oz (250 mL) jars of jam or marmalade; $1/2$ inch (1 cm) for 8-oz (250 mL) jars of chutney or relish, or pint (500 mL) or quart (1 L) jars of canned fruit or pickles. Remove any air bubbles using a nonmetallic instrument, and wipe the jar rims clean with a moist paper towel. Place the lids on the jars and screw the screwbands on until "fingertip-tight," meaning just until resistance is met. The screwband needs to keep the lid on, but the air must be able to escape the jar to create a seal.

5. Place the filled jars in the large pot, being careful not to overcrowd them and making sure they are covered with at least 2 inches (5 cm) of hot water. Make sure it's hot! Placing hot jars in cold water can cause thermal shock and break the jars. (Conversely, if you plunge your jars straight into boiling water, they can also break, as they will have cooled slightly unless you work at the speed of light.) Cover the pot and turn the heat on high. When the pot comes to a rolling boil, start a timer and let the jars process for the amount of time specified in the recipe (generally 5 to 10 minutes for jams and chutneys; longer for canned fruits or pickles in larger jars). You can turn down the heat a little if the water is boiling too wildly — no need to get the floor all wet!

6. When the timer goes off, turn off the heat and remove the lid, but let the jars rest in the water for 5 minutes before removing them to a folded tea towel or baking rack (again, to avoid thermal shock) on a spot on the counter where they can sit undisturbed for 24 hours. Soon you will hear the satisfying sound of the lids popping, creating their airtight seal. Before you store your jars, make sure all the jars have sealed properly.

If there are any that haven't, just store them in the fridge. It's best to store all preserves without the screwbands on, as these can rust.

As I mentioned, processing in a boiling water canner is a very important step, but don't think it's better to process for longer! The contents won't be safer — instead, you'll have overcooked fruit or mushy pickles. If you're making jam, prolonged exposure to heat can actually cause the pectin to break down, meaning the jam will lose its gel. The goal of processing is to get the center of the jar to the temperature of boiling water, which will stop or destroy any bacteria, mold, yeast or enzymes, as the growth of any of these could ruin your preserve.

A NOTE ON MEASUREMENTS

The imperial and metric equivalents used in these recipes are not rounded, as is typical; rather, they are converted more precisely. The precise amounts ensure that the balance of ingredients is correct for these preserving recipes. When measuring ingredients for a recipe, it is important to use all imperial measures or all metric measures to keep the ingredients in the right proportions. Do not use a mix of imperial and metric measures.

A NOTE ON COOKING TIMES

Where cooking times are given in a recipe, please know that they are approximations. This is less true of the recipes for baked goods in the last chapter, but for jams and their ilk there are so many variables at play that it's best to rely on the look and feel of the preserve more than on the time elapsed. The size and shape of your pot, the power of your stove, the water content of your fruit — all that and more can affect how long it takes for a preserve to reach doneness. Trust your own good judgment, which will improve with every batch you make, more than the clock!

EQUIPMENT

You don't need any fancy equipment to can, but there are a few pieces of equipment that are pretty indispensable if you're doing it a lot.

BARE MINIMUM

- ◇ THREE POTS (SMALL, BIG AND BIGGER): You'll need one for heating the lids, if doing so, one for cooking the preserve and a large one to use as a boiling water canner.
- ◇ CANNING JARS WITH TWO-PIECE LIDS: This seems obvious, but make sure you are using mason jars that are in good condition (not chipped or with a cracked rim). The screwbands should be free of rust and the snap lids new.
- ◇ PAPER TOWELS: You'll need them on hand for cleaning the jar rims.
- ◇ SPATULA: To get every last drop into the jars.
- ◇ DISH TOWEL OR METAL RACK: To place in the bottom of your pot when you heat-process.
- ◇ MEASURING CUPS AND SPOONS: I measure liquids using graded measuring cups with a pouring spout. For solids, I use nested cups that allow me to easily level the top. For both dry and liquid ingredients, amounts under $\frac{1}{4}$ cup (60 mL) should be measured with measuring spoons.

HIGHLY RECOMMENDED

◊ LADLE: This will help you get the jam or brine to the jar from the pot with ease.

◊ KITCHEN SCALE: Please get a scale — even a cheap one. It's the only way to be precise with measurements and ensure success with a recipe. If I tell you 6 Seville oranges, there could be a substantial difference between the weight of my oranges and yours. But if I tell you 2.2 lbs (1 kg) of oranges, there's no possibility of discrepancy.

◊ CANNING FUNNEL: This little number will make your life so much easier — its wide mouth keeps jar rims clean and prevents spillage.

◊ JAR LIFTER: A lifter is really helpful for removing jars upright from the hot-water bath. If you don't have one, just make sure to use something non-metallic to avoid scratching your jars.

◊ MAGNETIC WAND: This tool will help you get your snap lids out of their hot-water bath if you're heating the lids. You could theoretically make your own with a magnet and a chopstick; just make sure you don't use anything metallic that could scratch your lids.

◊ AIR BUBBLE REMOVER: This handy item helps you remove air bubbles (again, don't use anything metallic in its place!) and flips over for use as a handy headspace measure. Removing air bubbles is important — too much hidden air in a jar can disrupt the headspace and prevent your jars from sealing.

EXTRA CREDIT

◊ PRESERVING PAN: A copper preserving pan is the ultimate vessel for making jams, jellies and marmalades — copper is an amazing heat conductor, and the shape of the pan allows a maximum surface area for evaporation, meaning the jam can reduce faster. Unfortunately, copper cookware can be prohibitively expensive. It's possible to find less expensive stainless steel preserving pans (also known as maslin pans), but if you're a part-time jam-maker, a regular pot (the wider the better!) is a fine vessel. If you do use a copper pan, always mix your fruit with the sugar before putting it in the pan. Copper reacts with acid, and sugar prevents this from happening.

JAMS

❧

JAMS

"Comme le monde serait triste sans l'odeur des confitures."

— GEORGES DUHAMEL

Jams are, for the most part, a mixture of chopped fruit, sugar and lemon juice. Many recipes call for pectin, but I generally prefer not to use it. In fact, commercial pectin use is considered quite gauche in the artisan preserves community. High-pectin fruits, such as currants, cranberries and plums, will gel easily. Fruits lower in pectin can be helped along by the addition of lemon juice, a high-pectin apple or even boiled citrus fruit, but almost all fruits can easily reach a nice setting point without the addition of store-bought pectin.

Some jam-makers make their own pectin, using apples or oranges. Frankly, that has always seemed a little too high-maintenance for me. You will, however, find a few recipes that call for jam sugar (also known as gelling sugar or jelly sugar) — a sugar that already has pectin mixed in — as I use it occasionally to give a boost to low-pectin jams. Feel free to use regular granulated sugar instead if you are comfortable with a looser set. In North America we're accustomed to mass-produced jams and jellies with a very firm texture and more pectin and sugar than fruit. It's time to get used to a looser, "European-style" set. I prefer this set in low-pectin jams over adding pectin to achieve a firm set.

HIGH-PECTIN FRUITS
Apples, citrus fruits, crabapples, cranberries, currants, gooseberries, plums, quince

LOW-PECTIN FRUITS
Figs, nectarines, peaches, pears, rhubarb, strawberries, sweet cherries

At the market I often see old flats of strawberries for sale, labeled "jam strawberries." Avoid using overripe fruit for jam! The riper the fruit, the lower it is in pectin. The ideal for jam is a mixture of 25% slightly underripe and 75% perfectly ripe fruit.

Jam-making isn't all that complicated — it's really just a matter of proportions. Sugar helps jams gel and preserves the texture, color and flavor of the fruit over time, though if you add too much sugar, the flavor of the fruit cannot come through. The higher the sugar content, the longer the jam will keep, both in the pantry and once opened. What I am always after is balance: just enough sugar to balance the acidity of the fruit. Depending on the fruit, add 30% to 50% of the weight of the prepared fruit in sugar. This is much less sugar than most commercial and even homemade jams contain. Even so, a jam containing this much sugar should keep in the refrigerator for up to 1 year once opened. A jam that is very low in sugar may only keep for a few weeks or months.

As a rule, add 3 tbsp (45 mL) lemon juice per 2.2 lbs (1 kg) of fruit, which is about the juice of one lemon. You can use freshly squeezed juice unless the recipe specifically calls for bottled lemon juice. While the acidity might vary from one lemon to another, bottled lemon juice has a constant pH, so when a recipe calls for it, you must use it to obtain a safe pH. Most fruits are safe to can without additional acid, but lemon juice also draws pectin from fruit, helps with the set and balances the sugar, so I rarely make jam without it. Make sure to always add it when using low-acid fruits, such as bananas, figs, melons and papaya.

Many fruits benefit from a period of maceration, where you mix them with the sugar and lemon juice and let them stand, covered, for anywhere from 30 minutes to overnight before cooking. (They can also be refrigerated in an airtight container for up to 1 week.) The sugar draws the juices from the fruit, and together they become a syrup.

After maceration, the jam is cooked over medium-high heat until the setting point is reached. (It's difficult to say exactly how long this will take, since it depends on your equipment and other variables, but the jam recipes in this book should take between 15 and 25 minutes.) There are a few different ways to check the setting point. Eventually you will be able to tell if a jam is ready just by looking at it — the bubbles, the way it falls off the spatula — but that takes time and experience. When you're starting out, the best way to check a jam for doneness (and whenever you're in doubt) is the freezer plate method, which also works for marmalades and jellies. Put a small plate in the freezer when you start cutting up your fruit for jam (or just keep one in there at all times if you are doing a lot of canning). When the jam starts to look ready — the foam will subside, the jam will start to thicken and "sheet" off a spatula held aloft, and the bubbles will enlarge and look like fish eyes — put a teaspoon (5 mL) of jam on the plate and return it to the freezer for 2 minutes. (Remove the jam from the heat during this waiting period if it seems very close to being done. You can return it to the heat if it requires more cooking, but overcooking is impossible to undo.) After the 2 minutes, if the jam wrinkles like a silk shirt on the floor when pushed with your finger, it is ready. If not, boil it for another 5 minutes, then try again.

Once the setting point has been reached, remove the jam from the heat and let it rest for 5 minutes, stirring occasionally. This will prevent separation (a layer of fruit sitting unattractively atop a layer of jelly).

If you're planning on making a lot of jams, say for holiday gifts or another special event, do not make the mistake of making a triple or quadruple batch of a recipe. The cooking time will not just triple or quadruple but will increase exponentially! You will find yourself setting the alarm to get up and stir in the middle of the night. It is also much more difficult to determine the set with larger batches, even if you are experienced. You are better off to make multiple batches one after the other.

That way, there's always room in the canner, too. It sounds illogical, but trust me, it'll go faster.

Jams will keep, unopened, for 1 year. They will still be edible after that, but they will begin to discolor and the texture will change (not for the better).

A final note: let things mellow out before you declare defeat. The first time I made the Strawberry Margarita Jam (page 29), I thought I'd failed completely. Lo and behold, 3 weeks later I opened up the jar and was bewitched! It was so good. Just like pickles, jams sometimes need time to develop before consumption.

CHECKING DONENESS WITH A THERMOMETER

Some people use a thermometer to determine whether a jam is done, but for me that takes away all the fun of observing the jam's transformation. When there's a thermometer in the pot, people usually look a lot more at it than at the jam, even to the extent that they will let the jam burn if the thermometer doesn't yet register the right number! It's better just to be present and watchful.

BAKED APPLE JAM

THIS IS A RIFF ON famed jam-maker Christine Ferber's L'Autrichienne. It really evokes one of my favorite childhood desserts: apples hollowed out, filled with raisins, nuts and brown sugar, and baked to yielding perfection. Of course, I am an adult now, so there is also a healthy dose of rum. Think of it as dessert in a jar but also as a totally valid breakfast option. The Nuc, my former bandmate and this jam's #1 fan, likes it on his morning cereal. If possible, use freshly ground Ceylon cinnamon.

MAKES FOUR OR FIVE JARS (8 OZ/250 ML EACH)

2.6 lbs	apples (7 to 8 medium)	1.2 kg
1½ cups	granulated sugar	300 g
1¼ cups	packed brown sugar	265 g
3 tbsp	lemon juice	45 mL
1	vanilla bean, split and scraped	1
½ cup	raisins	100 g
¼ cup	dark rum	60 mL
1 tsp	ground cinnamon	5 mL
¾ cup	walnut pieces	150 g

Peel and core the apples, then slice them as thinly as possible.

In a large pot or preserving pan, combine the apples, granulated sugar, brown sugar, lemon juice and vanilla bean. Bring to a boil over medium-high heat, then transfer to a heatproof bowl, place a circle of parchment paper directly on the surface and refrigerate overnight.

Meanwhile, place the raisins in a jar and pour rum over top. Cover and let soak overnight.

The next day, prepare the jars and lids.

Return the apple mixture to the pot and bring to a boil over medium-high heat. Add the rum-soaked raisins and cinnamon. Return to a boil and cook for 5 minutes, then add the walnut pieces. Continue to boil until the jam becomes a very thick syrup that is very much overshadowed by fruit. (Note that this jam does not reach the same setting point as others.) Remove from heat and let rest for 5 minutes, stirring occasionally. Remove the vanilla bean (see tip, at left).

Ladle jam into the hot jars to within ¼ inch (0.5 cm) of the rim. Remove any air bubbles and wipe rims. Place the lids on the jars and screw the bands on until fingertip-tight. Process in a boiling water canner for 10 minutes.

VARIATION

If you prefer to omit the rum, plump the raisins in ¼ cup (60 mL) hot water or apple juice, and drain before using.

TIP

Don't throw out the vanilla bean after removing it from the jam! It still has lots of flavor. Rinse it and then leave it to dry out completely in a warm place (like on top of the oven), then tuck it into granulated sugar to make vanilla sugar, or save up a bunch and use them to infuse rum or vodka for homemade vanilla extract.

APRICOT JAM WITH HONEY AND CHAMOMILE

THIS JAM IS SUMMER. Fragrant apricots, honey and fresh chamomile flowers are an incredible trifecta of flavor. Try to use ripe apricots grown as nearby as possible, and a honey that complements their flavor (I always use Miel d'Anicet's raw honey). Substitute dried chamomile for the fresh if need be.

MAKES FIVE OR SIX JARS (8 OZ/250 ML EACH)

3.3 lbs	apricots (about 30 medium), chopped	1.5 kg
1¾ cups	granulated sugar	350 g
13 oz	honey	375 g
⅓ cup	lemon juice	75 mL
2 tbsp	fresh chamomile flowers	12 g

TIP
If you like, throw in a handful of extra chamomile flowers toward the end of cooking. This is solely for aesthetics, but it does look pretty.

In a large pot or preserving pan, combine the apricots, sugar, honey and lemon juice. Put the chamomile flowers in a mesh tea strainer, or tie them up in a bundle with cheesecloth, and add to the pot. Let stand briefly to macerate.

In the meantime, prepare the jars and lids.

Bring the apricot mixture to a boil over medium-high heat, stirring often. Boil hard, stirring often, until the setting point is reached (see page 17). Remove from heat and let rest for 5 minutes, stirring occasionally.

Ladle jam into the hot jars to within ¼ inch (0.5 cm) of the rim. Remove any air bubbles and wipe rims. Place the lids on the jars and screw the bands on until fingertip-tight. Process in a boiling water canner for 10 minutes.

FIG JAM WITH SECRETS

I FIRST INVENTED THIS JAM BACK IN 2006. Truth be told, I can't remember what the "secrets" were back then, but the new ones are perfect. Of course I enjoy the coyness of the name, but what's really cool about it is that the secret ingredients — orange, vanilla bean, cinnamon and Amaro Nonino (an Italian bitter) — seamlessly enhance the taste of the figs. It's like you don't even know they're there — the figs just taste, well, better. Figgier, even! My assistant, Ariane, says this jam looks like a starry night sky, which is perfectly, poetically apt, and just one more reason to make it as soon as possible.

MAKES ABOUT SIX JARS (8 OZ/250 ML EACH)

3.3 lbs	fresh black figs (about 25 large)	1.5 kg
3¼ cups + 2 tbsp	granulated sugar	675 g
	Grated zest and juice of 1 orange	
½ cup	bottled lemon juice	125 mL
1	vanilla bean, split and scraped	1
1	1-inch (2.5 cm) piece cinnamon stick (preferably Ceylon)	1
¼ cup	Amaro Nonino liqueur	60 mL

Remove the stems and coarsely chop the figs. You should have about 7½ cups (1.875 L).

In a large pot or preserving pan, combine the figs, sugar, orange zest and juice, lemon juice and vanilla bean. Crumble in Ceylon cinnamon or, if using cassia cinnamon, just throw in the stick. Cover and let stand to macerate for anywhere from 30 minutes to overnight (or refrigerate in an airtight container for up to 1 week).

In the meantime, prepare the jars and lids.

Bring the fig mixture to a boil over medium-high heat, stirring often. Boil hard, stirring often, until the setting point is reached (see page 17). Remove from heat and let rest for 5 minutes, stirring occasionally. Remove the vanilla bean (see tip, page 20) and cassia cinnamon (if using).

Ladle jam into the hot jars to within ¼ inch (0.5 cm) of the rim. Remove any air bubbles and wipe rims. Place the lids on the jars and screw the bands on until fingertip-tight. Process in a boiling water canner for 10 minutes.

TIPS

Do not substitute freshly squeezed lemon juice in this recipe. While acidity varies from one lemon to another, bottled lemon juice has a constant pH and will ensure a safe pH level for these figs, which are a low-acid fruit.

If you can find Ceylon cinnamon, splurge on it. Most cinnamon sold in the grocery store is cassia cinnamon. Ceylon cinnamon is softer, almost crumbly, and I prefer its flavor. You can find it in quality spice stores or gourmet shops.

PLUM JAM WITH STAR ANISE

FOR WHATEVER REASON, plums go very well with the black licorice flavor of star anise. I make this jam for Vieux Velo, the café down the street from my old workshop, and it is the jam most requested by staff. While any plum will work, I tend to use the common purple-skinned, yellow-fleshed variety.

MAKES ABOUT FIVE JARS (8 OZ/250 ML EACH)

2.4 lbs	plums (about 13 medium)	1.1 kg
2 cups	granulated sugar	400 g
3 tbsp	lemon juice	45 mL
1	whole star anise	1

Chop the plums into small pieces. (Depending on their ripeness, they won't break down that much, so the smaller the pieces, the more uniform your jam will be.)

In a large pot or preserving pan, combine the plums, sugar, lemon juice and star anise. Cover and let stand to macerate for anywhere from 30 minutes to overnight (or refrigerate in an airtight container for up to 1 week).

In the meantime, prepare the jars and lids.

Bring the plum mixture to a boil over medium-high heat, stirring often. Boil hard, stirring often, until the setting point is reached (see page 17). Remove from heat and let rest for 5 minutes, stirring occasionally. Discard the star anise.

Ladle jam into the hot jars to within ¼ inch (0.5 cm) of the rim. Remove any air bubbles and wipe rims. Place the lids on the jars and screw the bands on until fingertip-tight. Process in a boiling water canner for 10 minutes.

PEACH JAM WITH BOURBON AND HONEY

THIS IS ONE OF MY ABSOLUTE FAVORITE JAMS. Make sure to use fragrant peaches grown as nearby as possible (preferably freestone, as they're easier to pit), as well as an excellent honey. I use organic raw honey from Miel d'Anicet, for its superlative flavor. Avoid using a honey that is too strong-tasting, like buckwheat honey, or a too subtle one whose perfume might be lost.

MAKES ABOUT FIVE JARS (8 OZ/250 ML EACH)

2.4 lbs	peaches (about 8 medium)	1.1 kg
1¼ cups	granulated sugar	250 g
9 oz	honey	250 g
3 tbsp	lemon juice	45 mL
2 tbsp	bourbon	30 mL

Chop the peaches into small pieces. (Depending on their ripeness, they won't break down that much, so the smaller the pieces, the more uniform your jam will be.)

In a large pot or preserving pan, combine the peaches, sugar, honey and lemon juice. Cover and let stand to macerate for anywhere from 30 minutes to overnight (or refrigerate in an airtight container for up to 1 week).

In the meantime, prepare the jars and lids.

Bring the peach mixture to a boil over medium-high heat, stirring often. Boil hard, stirring often, until the setting point is reached (see page 17). Remove from heat and let rest for 5 minutes, stirring occasionally. Stir in the bourbon.

Ladle jam into the hot jars to within ¼ inch (0.5 cm) of the rim. Remove any air bubbles and wipe rims. Place the lids on the jars and screw the bands on until fingertip-tight. Process in a boiling water canner for 10 minutes.

PUR CASSIS

SIMPLE AS IT IS, this is my favorite jam of all. I always use black currants I picked myself (often with the help of friends), and I find they need no embellishment — their musky perfume and whole-berry, seedy texture is perfection. This jam is absolutely covetable.

MAKES ABOUT FIVE JARS (8 OZ/250 ML EACH)

2.7 lbs	black currants	1.2 kg
3 cups	granulated sugar	600 g
¼ cup	lemon juice	60 mL

TIP

If you don't have a kitchen scale, you'll need 8 cups (1.9 L) black currants for this recipe.

In a large pot or preserving pan, combine the black currants, sugar and lemon juice. Bring to a boil over medium-high heat, stirring often. As soon as it begins to boil, transfer to a heatproof bowl, place a round of parchment paper directly on the surface and refrigerate overnight.

The next day, prepare the jars and lids.

Return the black currant mixture to the pot and bring to a boil over medium-high heat, stirring often. Boil hard, stirring often, until the setting point is reached (see page 17). Remove from heat and let rest for 5 minutes, stirring occasionally.

Ladle jam into the hot jars to within ¼ inch (0.5 cm) of the rim. Remove any air bubbles and wipe rims. Place the lids on the jars and screw the bands on until fingertip-tight. Process in a boiling water canner for 10 minutes.

REALLY GOOD RASPBERRY JAM

IN THE FRENCH VERSION OF THIS BOOK, I boasted that it wasn't just another canning book with just another recipe for raspberry jam. But you know what? Raspberry jam is good. And while there are a lot of recipes out there, they vary wildly, so it's good to have one in your pocket that you *know* is really good. This one is. I make a batch for myself at least once a year.

MAKES FOUR OR FIVE JARS (8 OZ/250 ML EACH)

2.8 lbs	raspberries	1.25 kg
3 cups	granulated sugar	600 g
3 tbsp	lemon juice	45 mL

TIP

If you don't have a kitchen scale, you'll need 11 cups (2.6 L) raspberries for this recipe.

In a large pot or preserving pan, combine the raspberries, sugar and lemon juice. Let stand to macerate for anywhere from 15 minutes to overnight (or refrigerate in an airtight container for up to 1 week). (I don't crush my berries at all because I love the chunky texture. They will break down some on their own anyway. If you prefer a smooth jam, crush them now — with your hands!)

In the meantime, prepare the jars and lids.

Bring the raspberry mixture to a boil over medium-high heat, stirring often. Boil hard, stirring often, until the setting point is reached (see page 17). Remove from heat and let rest for 5 minutes, stirring occasionally.

Ladle jam into the hot jars to within ¼ inch (0.5 cm) of the rim. Remove any air bubbles and wipe rims. Place the lids on the jars and screw the bands on until fingertip-tight. Process in a boiling water canner for 10 minutes.

VARIATION

If you're wanting something a little different, try adding a handful of cocoa nibs for a chocolaty crunch. Add them once the raspberry mixture is boiling.

STRAWBERRY MARGARITA JAM

I DEVELOPED THIS RECIPE for a *Globe and Mail* article on spring canning. I thought it was a one-off, but a few weeks later I spread the test batch on my toast and did not stop eating it until the jar was empty. It seemed like I should probably put it into production. This is a bright, complex strawberry preserve that tastes very good with bread and butter but could effortlessly glide into a more sophisticated milieu.

MAKES ABOUT SEVEN JARS (8 OZ/250 ML EACH)

10.5 oz	limes (about 3 medium)	300 g
3 cups	water	750 mL
3.3 lbs	strawberries	1.5 kg
4¼ cups	granulated sugar	850 g
6 tbsp	lemon juice	90 mL
2 tsp	kosher salt	10 mL
1 tsp	citric acid	5 mL
⅓ cup	silver tequila	75 mL
3 tbsp	triple sec	45 mL

TIPS

If you don't have a kitchen scale, you'll need 9¾ cups (2.3 L) halved hulled strawberries (or quartered, if large) for this recipe.

If using fresh lemon juice, you'll need about 2 lemons for 6 tbsp (90 mL) lemon juice.

It's best to let this jam mellow out a bit and let the flavors meld before eating it. Try to wait at least 2 weeks.

Quarter the limes lengthwise and slice them as thinly as possible. Place them in a bowl with the water and let soak overnight.

The next day, transfer the limes and water to a heavy saucepan. Bring to a boil, then reduce the heat and simmer until the limes are tender and most of the water has evaporated, about 1 hour.

Meanwhile, hull and halve the strawberries (or quarter them, if large), and mix with the sugar in a large bowl. Let stand to macerate until the limes are ready.

In the meantime, prepare the jars and lids.

When the limes are ready, add the strawberry-sugar mixture and the lemon juice. Increase heat to medium-high and bring to a boil, stirring often. Boil hard, stirring often, until froth subsides and bubbles become regular and sputter violently. Test jam for doneness (see page 17). When the setting point is reached, remove from heat and stir in the salt and citric acid. Let rest for 5 minutes, stirring occasionally. Stir in the tequila and triple sec.

Ladle jam into the hot jars to within ¼ inch (0.5 cm) of the rim. Remove any air bubbles and wipe rims. Place the lids on the jars and screw the bands on until fingertip-tight. Process in a boiling water canner for 10 minutes.

BANANAS FOSTER JAM

THIS JAM IS A TAKE on the classic New Orleans dessert of bananas flambéed with rum and served over ice cream. For some reason you don't often see bananas made into jam, as ubiquitous as they are. Make sure you use ripe bananas or the texture will be disappointingly weird. The butter extract isn't necessary, but use it if you, like me, want to be true to all the flavors of the original.

MAKES ABOUT EIGHT JARS (8 OZ/250 ML EACH)

5.9 lbs	ripe bananas	2.7 kg
2¼ cups	packed brown sugar	500 g
1 cup	jam (gelling) sugar	200 g
½ tsp	ground cinnamon	2 mL
⅔ cup	bottled lemon juice	150 mL
¼ cup	dark rum, divided	60 mL
1	vanilla bean, split and scraped	1
¼ tsp	butter extract (optional)	1 mL

Prepare the jars and lids.

Peel and dice bananas, then weigh out 4.2 lbs (1.9 kg) or measure 12⅔ cups (3 L).

In a large pot or preserving pan, combine the bananas, brown sugar, jam sugar, cinnamon, lemon juice, half the rum and the vanilla bean. Bring to a boil over medium-high heat, stirring often. Boil hard, stirring often, until the setting point is reached (see page 17). Remove from heat and let rest for 5 minutes, stirring occasionally. Add the remaining rum and the butter extract (if using), stirring well. Remove the vanilla bean (see tip, page 20).

Ladle jam into the hot jars to within ¼ inch (0.5 cm) of the rim. Remove any air bubbles and wipe rims. Place the lids on the jars and screw the bands on until fingertip-tight. Process in a boiling water canner for 10 minutes.

> **TIP**
>
> Do not substitute freshly squeezed lemon juice in this recipe. While acidity varies from one lemon to another, bottled lemon juice has a constant pH and will ensure a safe pH level for these bananas, which are a low-acid fruit.

INDUSTRIAL REVOLUTION ENGLAND 1844

IN 2007 I WAS LUCKY ENOUGH to tour with one of my favorite bands, Xiu Xiu. It was such a thrill to see them perform every night — their front man, Jamie Stewart, is brilliant. Some years later, having left music for preserves, I was really feeling the absence of that other sort of creativity in my life. I came up with an idea to get artists I liked to invent wild jam ideas that I would bring to life. The two from Jamie — this one and French Revolution, 1789 — are the only ones that ever came to fruition, but they're both incredibly good.

MAKES ABOUT SIX JARS (8 OZ/250 ML EACH)

1.1 lbs	blackberries	500 g
1.1 lbs	blueberries	500 g
1.1 lbs	black currants	500 g
3 cups	granulated sugar	600 g
3 tbsp	lemon juice	45 mL
8	firm medium black plums	8
1/3 cup	candied ginger, finely diced	75 g
2 tbsp	black tea leaves	10 g
1/2 cup	gin	125 mL

TIPS

If you don't have a kitchen scale, you'll need 4⅓ cups (1.08 L) of each of the blackberries and blueberries and 3 cups (750 mL) black currants for this recipe.

Use any black tea you like, but I prefer Monk's Blend — its fruitiness blends seamlessly into the whole.

In a large pot or preserving pan, combine the blackberries, blueberries, black currants, sugar and lemon juice.

Peel the plums and chop the peels medium-fine so that they resemble confetti (reserve the plum flesh for another use). Add the plum peels to the pot, along with the ginger and tea leaves. Let stand to macerate for 1 hour.

In the meantime, prepare the jars and lids.

Bring the plum peel mixture to a boil over medium-high heat, stirring often. Boil hard, stirring often, until the setting point is reached (see page 17). Remove from heat and let rest for 5 minutes, stirring occasionally. Add the gin, stirring well.

Ladle jam into the hot jars to within ¼ inch (0.5 cm) of the rim. Remove any air bubbles and wipe rims. Place the lids on the jars and screw the bands on until fingertip-tight. Process in a boiling water canner for 10 minutes.

FRENCH REVOLUTION 1789

THIS IS THE SISTER JAM to Industrial Revolution, England, 1844. They make an excellent pair. Don't use the best champagne in this — an affordable cava is just fine. But make sure to use one you would still want to drink! The flavor will come through in the jam and, besides, there'll be some left over. (Or you could purchase a mini bottle, which at 8 oz/250 mL is the perfect amount for this recipe.)

MAKES ABOUT FIVE JARS (8 OZ/250 ML EACH)

1.1 lbs	stemmed red currants	500 g
1.1 lbs	pitted sour cherries	500 g
1.1 lbs	beheaded strawberries, halved (or quartered, if large)	500 g
3⅓ cups	granulated sugar	675 g
⅓ cup	lemon juice	75 mL
2	vanilla beans, split and scraped	2
	Handful of edible red rose petals or 2 tsp (10 mL) rose water	
1 cup	sparkling wine, divided	250 mL

Prepare the jars and lids.

In a large pot or preserving pan, combine the red currants, cherries, strawberries, sugar, lemon juice and vanilla beans. If using rose petals, add them now. Add half the sparkling wine. Bring to a boil over medium-high heat, stirring often. Boil hard, stirring often, until the setting point is reached (see page 17). Remove from heat and let rest for 5 minutes, stirring occasionally. Remove the vanilla beans (see tip, page 20). If using rose water, add it now. Stir in the remaining sparkling wine.

Ladle jam into the hot jars to within ¼ inch (0.5 cm) of the rim. Remove any air bubbles and wipe rims. Place the lids on the jars and screw the bands on until fingertip-tight. Process in a boiling water canner for 10 minutes.

> ### TIP
> If you don't have a kitchen scale, you'll need 3 cups (750 mL) stemmed red currants, 3¼ cups (800 mL) pitted sour cherries and 3¼ cups (800 mL) halved hulled strawberries (or quartered, if large) for this recipe.

PIÑA COLADA JAM

THIS DELICIOUS JAM SPEAKS FOR ITSELF. It's got all the flavors of the classic cocktail, but is socially acceptable to eat for breakfast. The chunky texture, full of chewy coconut, also makes it a pretty choice for a dessert component — on ice cream, between cake layers, stirred into mascarpone … the list goes on.

MAKES ABOUT FIVE JARS (8 OZ/250 ML EACH)

2.9 lbs	pineapple flesh (from 2 pineapples)	1.3 kg
2½ cups	jam (gelling) sugar	500 g
1⅔ cups	unsweetened flaked coconut	100 g
	Grated zest and juice of 2 limes	
6 tbsp	dark rum, divided	90 mL

Chop the pineapple into fairly small dice.

In a large pot or preserving pan, combine the pineapple, sugar, coconut, lime zest and juice and about half the rum. Cover and let stand to macerate for 30 minutes.

In the meantime, prepare the jars and lids.

Bring the pineapple mixture to a boil over medium-high heat, stirring often. Boil hard, stirring often, until the setting point is reached (see page 17). Remove from heat and let rest for 5 minutes, stirring occasionally. Stir in the remaining rum.

Ladle jam into the hot jars to within ¼ inch (0.5 cm) of the rim. Remove any air bubbles and wipe rims. Place the lids on the jars and screw the bands on until fingertip-tight. Process in a boiling water canner for 10 minutes.

BLUEBARB JAM

A RECIPE FOR RHUBARB AND BLUEBERRY PIE inspired this jam recipe, which makes it a shoe-in filling for the Jam Pockets on page 170. I suppose it's a common enough flavor, but it seemed inspired the first time I caught wind of it. Blueberries appear in Quebec when rhubarb is just winding down, and this jam is a perfect way to prolong the summer. I tend to find blueberry jam somewhat insipid — here, the addition of tart red rhubarb, one of my true loves, is transformative.

MAKES SIX OR SEVEN JARS (8 OZ/250 ML EACH)

2.2 lbs	rhubarb, chopped	1 kg
1.1 lbs	blueberries	500 g
4¼ cups	granulated sugar	850 g
⅓ cup	lemon juice	75 mL

TIP

If you don't have a kitchen scale, you'll need 7 cups (1.75 L) chopped rhubarb and 4¼ cups (800 mL) blueberries for this recipe.

Prepare the jars and lids.

In a large pot or preserving pan, combine the rhubarb, blueberries, sugar and lemon juice. Cover and let stand to macerate for anywhere from 30 minutes to overnight (or refrigerate in an airtight container for up to 1 week).

Bring the rhubarb mixture to a boil over medium-high heat, stirring often. Boil hard, stirring often, until the setting point is reached (see page 17). Remove from heat and let rest for 5 minutes, stirring occasionally.

Ladle jam into the hot jars to within ¼ inch (0.5 cm) of the rim. Remove any air bubbles and wipe rims. Place the lids on the jars and screw the bands on until fingertip-tight. Process in a boiling water canner for 10 minutes.

STRAWBERRY RHUBARB JAM

THIS IS A CLASSIC — one to make when the first strawberries arrive and before the precious rhubarb disappears! The tart rhubarb is a perfect foil to the sweet strawberries, and though the vanilla bean is optional, I highly recommend it.

MAKES ABOUT EIGHT JARS (8 OZ/250 ML EACH)

2.7 lbs	rhubarb, roughly chopped	1.2 kg
1.5 lbs	hulled strawberries, halved (or quartered, if large)	660 g
1	green apple (about 6 oz/180 g), peeled and finely chopped	1
5 cups	granulated sugar	1 kg
⅔ cup	lemon juice	150 mL
½	vanilla bean (optional), scraped	½

TIPS

If you don't have a kitchen scale, you'll need 8¾ cups (2.1 L) roughly chopped rhubarb and 4½ cups (1.125 L) halved hulled strawberries (or quartered, if large) for this recipe.

If using fresh lemon juice, you'll need about 3½ lemons for ⅔ cup (150 mL) lemon juice.

In a large pot or preserving pan, combine the rhubarb, strawberries, apple, sugar, lemon juice and vanilla bean (if using). Cover and let stand to macerate for anywhere from 30 minutes to overnight (or refrigerate in an airtight container for up to 1 week).

In the meantime, prepare the jars and lids.

Bring the rhubarb mixture to a boil over medium-high heat, stirring often. Boil hard, stirring often, until the setting point is reached (see page 17). Remove from heat and let rest for 5 minutes, stirring occasionally. Remove the vanilla bean (if using).

Ladle jam into the hot jars to within ¼ inch (0.5 cm) of the rim. Remove any air bubbles and wipe rims. Place the lids on the jars and screw the bands on until fingertip-tight. Process in a boiling water canner for 10 minutes.

PEACH PASSION FRUIT JAM

THIS IS A BEAUTIFUL JAM — bright orange flecked with little black orbs, which crunch delightfully. If you are not a fan of crunch, however, feel free to remove the seeds by straining the passion fruit pulp before combining it with the other ingredients.

MAKES FIVE OR SIX JARS (8 OZ/250 ML EACH)

3.3 lbs	peaches (7 to 8 large)	1.5 kg
1 cup	passion fruit pulp (see tip, below)	225 g
⅔ cup	thawed frozen passion fruit purée or passion fruit juice (optional)	150 mL
4 cups	granulated sugar	800 g
6 tbsp	lemon juice	90 mL

TIPS

You'll need 10 to 11 medium passion fruit to get 1 cup (225 g) pulp. If fresh passion fruit are not available, look for frozen pulp, often found at South American grocery stores. You might want to look for it anyway — it's more affordable than fresh passion fruit!

If you can find it, use thawed frozen passion fruit purée (from Ravifruit or Boiron) to add another layer of flavor. Passion fruit juice will work in a pinch. If you can't find either, the jam will still be delicious and very much worth making.

Chop the peaches into small pieces. (Depending on their ripeness, they won't break down that much, so the smaller the pieces, the more uniform your jam will be.)

In a large pot or preserving pan, combine the peaches, passion fruit pulp, passion fruit purée (if using), sugar and lemon juice. Cover and let stand to macerate for anywhere from 30 minutes to overnight (or refrigerate in an airtight container for up to 1 week).

In the meantime, prepare the jars and lids.

Bring the peach mixture to a boil over medium-high heat, stirring often. Boil hard, stirring often, until the setting point is reached (see page 17). Remove from heat and let rest for 5 minutes, stirring occasionally.

Ladle jam into the hot jars to within ¼ inch (0.5 cm) of the rim. Remove any air bubbles and wipe rims. Place the lids on the jars and screw the bands on until fingertip-tight. Process in a boiling water canner for 10 minutes.

RHUBARB BLOOD ORANGE JAM

THIS JAM IS BASED ON my company's rhubarb-grapefruit jam, which is based on a Chez Panisse recipe. I love that pairing, but this one might be even better. Rhubarb is often paired with orange, but I tend to find that combination flat and tiresome. The bitter tanginess of the blood orange with rhubarb, though — that is something else entirely.

Of course, rhubarb and blood oranges don't tend to appear at the same time of year (at least, not where I live, in Montreal), so you'll have to freeze one or the other ahead of time. Trust me, it's worth it.

Use a very red variety of rhubarb, and you'll have a shockingly crimson jam that you won't want to hide away in the cupboard.

MAKES ABOUT FOUR JARS (8 OZ/250 ML EACH)

1.2 lbs	blood oranges (about 3½ medium)	550 g
1.7 lbs	rhubarb, chopped	750 g
2½ cups	granulated sugar	500 g
3 tbsp	lemon juice	45 mL

TIP
If you don't have a kitchen scale, you'll need 5½ cups (1.375 L) chopped rhubarb for this recipe.

Using a vegetable peeler, remove all of the zest from the blood oranges in large strips, trying to remove as little of the white pith as possible. Stack the strips of zest and cut them finely across the short side to make a fine julienne. Juice the oranges.

In a large pot or preserving pan, combine the julienned zest, orange juice, rhubarb, sugar and lemon juice. Cover and let stand to macerate for anywhere from 30 minutes to overnight (or refrigerate in an airtight container for up to 1 week).

In the meantime, prepare the jars and lids.

Bring the orange zest mixture to a boil over medium-high heat, stirring often. Boil hard, stirring often, until the setting point is reached (see page 17). Remove from heat and let rest for 5 minutes, stirring occasionally.

Ladle jam into the hot jars to within ¼ inch (0.5 cm) of the rim. Remove any air bubbles and wipe rims. Place the lids on the jars and screw the bands on until fingertip-tight. Process in a boiling water canner for 10 minutes.

THREE RED FRUITS

IF YOU'VE THOUGHT TO FREEZE some red fruits during the summer months, this is a great jam to make during cranberry season in the fall, to get a head start on Christmas gifts. People love red jam, no doubt because it's what they're familiar with, so I created this right before the holiday season one year when I realized that my stranger tastes just weren't going to satisfy everyone.

Alternatively, you can make this jam in the summertime with frozen cranberries, which are easy to come by and tend to be of good quality. The texture is fantastic, the taste is well balanced, and the color pops no matter what the season.

MAKES ABOUT SIX JARS (8 OZ/250 ML EACH)

1.3 lbs	pitted sour cherries	575 g
1.3 lbs	cranberries	575 g
12.4 oz	raspberries	350 g
4¼ cups	granulated sugar	850 g
⅓ cup	lemon juice	75 mL

TIP

If you don't have a kitchen scale, you'll need 3¾ cups (925 mL) pitted sour cherries, 5 cups (1.25 L) cranberries and 3 cups (750 mL) raspberries for this recipe.

Prepare the jars and lids.

In a large pot or preserving pan, combine the cherries, cranberries, raspberries, sugar and lemon juice. Bring to a boil over medium-high heat, stirring often. Boil hard, stirring often and pressing the cranberries up against the side of the pan (this will force them to pop and make a more uniform jam), until the setting point is reached (see page 17). Remove from heat and let rest for 5 minutes, stirring occasionally.

Ladle jam into the hot jars to within ¼ inch (0.5 cm) of the rim. Remove any air bubbles and wipe rims. Place the lids on the jars and screw the bands on until fingertip-tight. Process in a boiling water canner for 10 minutes.

BLOOD AND SAND JAM

I CREATED THIS JAM for the Berlin-themed issue of an arts and culture magazine called *Citta*. It is based on the flavors of the cocktail Blood and Sand, a great version of which I drank once in New York City. How I drew a line from touring through Berlin to NYC is not important — the jam still tastes great. I am not a huge fan of navel oranges; if you can use Seville or blood oranges, please do, though the seasons may conspire against you. If you have the forethought, freeze a few Sevilles in February to make this in July. Note that, because the different oranges have different amounts of pectin, the set of the jam will vary based on which you choose — Sevilles will produce a firmer set, while navel or blood oranges will be softer.

MAKES ABOUT FIVE JARS (8 OZ/250 ML EACH)

2	medium oranges (about 15 oz/420 g)	2
2.2 lbs	black cherries	1 kg
2 cups	granulated sugar	400 g
6 tbsp	lemon juice	90 mL
¼ cup	Scotch	60 mL
2 tbsp	cherry brandy (preferably Cherry Heering)	30 mL
½ tsp	bitters (preferably orange)	2 mL

TIPS

If you don't have a kitchen scale, you'll need 7 cups (1.75 L) black cherries for this recipe.

If using fresh lemon juice, you'll need about 2 lemons for 6 tbsp (90 mL) lemon juice.

Place the oranges in a pot (yes, left whole, peel and all) and cover with water. Bring to a boil over high heat. Reduce the heat to medium-low, cover and simmer, stirring occasionally, until the oranges are quite soft, about 2 hours.

Meanwhile, stem, halve and pit the cherries. Combine them with the sugar and lemon juice in a large pot or preserving pan. Let stand to macerate until the oranges are ready.

In the meantime, prepare the jars and lids.

When the oranges are ready, transfer them to a cutting board and let cool a little. Reserve 2 tbsp (30 mL) of the cooking liquid and add it to the cherry mixture. Finely chop the oranges, discarding the stem ends and any seeds. Add the chopped oranges to the cherry mixture.

Bring the cherry mixture to a boil over medium-high heat, stirring often. Boil hard, stirring often, until the setting point is reached (see page 17). Remove from heat and let rest for 5 minutes, stirring occasionally. Add the Scotch, brandy and bitters, stirring well.

Ladle jam into the hot jars to within ¼ inch (0.5 cm) of the rim. Remove any air bubbles and wipe rims. Place the lids on the jars and screw the bands on until fingertip-tight. Process in a boiling water canner for 10 minutes.

MARMALADES

❧

MARMALADES

"Bitterness is the richest and most intellectually satisfying flavor that exists."

— ANDONI LUIS ADURIZ (MUGARITZ)

Full disclosure: I have failed at the International Marmalade Awards (yes, that's a thing) two years in a row. But I wouldn't change a thing. I love the marmalades I make, and happily I'm not alone. I think my poor performance is because I generally prefer what would be considered a homey marmalade: a good rough-cut spread containing more peel than jelly. I'm not entirely unrefined, though — one famous food writer didn't even bother to remove the seeds for his version!

Dating back to ancient Roman times, marmalade was first made with quince and called *chardequynce* or *quidony*. For centuries it was cooked to such a thick gel that it was conserved in boxes and served in slices, mostly as a dessert. It was the Scots who began to add more water, rendering it spreadable, and who consumed it at breakfast in lieu of the traditional dram of whisky (much to some breakfasters' dismay).

Over the centuries, in addition to a breakfast spread, marmalade has been considered a dessert, an aphrodisiac and a medicine.

True orange marmalade is considered by most to be that made with the Seville orange, a sour variety and the first to arrive in Europe. At first its pulp was beaten to make a smooth conserve, but the "chipped" style overtook this in popularity. As marmalade consumption increased and new varieties of citrus became available, the market offered an abundance of flavors and textures; thick-cut marmalade was considered men's fare, while fine-shred was suitable for ladies and children.

So how should you cut it? It all depends on personal taste, which may vary for every citrus variety. I typically make marmalade using either the whole fruit method or the sliced fruit method. The whole fruit method consists of boiling the citrus until it is quite soft, then slicing and mixing it with sugar right away. With the sliced fruit method, the fruit is sliced raw, soaked in water overnight, boiled down to tenderness and then made into marmalade. The whole fruit method tends to make a chunkier, more rustic preserve, while the sliced fruit method is a little more refined. I vary my approach depending on what citrus fruit I'm using.

It may seem like there is quite a lot of sugar in these recipes, but I actually tend to use a lot less than most marmalade-makers. And the fact of the matter is that we are making a sweet spread with bitter citrus peel and, especially in the case of the Seville orange, very sour citrus flesh. The amount of sugar only makes sense.

Testing for doneness is much the same as for jam (see page 17). As the foam subsides, you will see the bubbles become rhythmic and more organized. This is a sure sign that it is almost ready.

Processed marmalade will keep for at least 2 years on the shelf and is considered only to improve with age. While I enjoy both fresh and aged marmalade, my preference is a 1-year-old marmalade — its color is darker, its texture firmer and its scent and flavor richer. I always make sure to keep one jar for at least that long.

PIPS: TO BOIL OR NOT TO BOTHER?

Marmalade recipes often call for you to boil the seeds to extract their pectin. Citrus seeds do contain pectin, to be sure, but most of the pectin is contained in the peel. So is it worth boiling the seeds to extract pectin? It certainly can't hurt your gel, but in my experience it also won't make a significant difference. Personally, I don't bother.

"[Quince marmalades] cause good appetite, and preserveth the head from drunkenness ... and taken after the meat, it closeth and draweth the stomach together, and helpeth it to digest, and mollifyeth the belly, if it be abundantly taken."

— SIR THOMAS ELYOT, *THE CASTEL OF HELTH* (1541)

CLASSIC SEVILLE ORANGE MARMALADE

THIS IS THE PRESERVE that really defines marmalade for me, and it's my true love. My heart soars whenever I look at a jar of it, with its perfect set and hot orange hue. Sometimes I have to randomly stop what I'm doing in the workshop and go to the fridge and eat a spoonful. Seville oranges have a short season that begins in January and lasts until March at the latest. I try to make as much marmalade with them as I possibly can during this brief window. I like my peel cut pretty chunky, but you are free to do as you please.

MAKES ABOUT FIVE JARS (8 OZ/250 ML EACH)

2.2 lbs	Seville oranges (about 6)	1 kg
5¼ cups	granulated sugar	1.05 kg
6 tbsp	lemon juice	90 mL
½ cup	water	125 mL

TIPS

Because this recipe uses whole oranges, it is better to have slightly more than the weight called for than it is to have slightly less. Use the number of oranges that allows you to meet or slightly exceed 2.2 lbs (1 kg).

When you're simmering the oranges, check the water level occasionally and add hot water from a kettle if it reduces too much.

Place the oranges in a large pot and add enough water so that they float freely. Cover and bring to a boil over high heat. Reduce the heat to medium and simmer for about 2 hours or until quite soft (they will begin to collapse).

Drain the oranges, transfer them to a cutting board and let cool until you can handle them. Chop them to desired thickness, discarding the stem end and seeds.

In a large pot or preserving pan, combine the chopped oranges, sugar and lemon juice. Cover and let stand to macerate overnight. (The orange mixture will gel slightly as it macerates.)

The next day, prepare the jars and lids.

Add the water to the orange mixture and bring to a boil over medium-high heat, stirring often. Boil hard, stirring often, until the setting point is reached (see page 17). Remove from heat and let rest for 5 minutes, stirring occasionally.

Ladle marmalade into the hot jars to within ¼ inch (0.5 cm) of the rim. Remove any air bubbles and wipe rims. Place the lids on the jars and screw the bands on until fingertip-tight. Process in a boiling water canner for 10 minutes.

CREAM POP MARMALADE

THIS MARMALADE IS MEANT to recall Creamsicles: the frozen treat of vanilla ice cream encased in a layer of orange Popsicle. I find clementines most closely approximate that candy-sweet orange Popsicle flavor, while white chocolate and vanilla bean are meant to mimic the ice cream.

MAKES ABOUT SIX JARS (8 OZ/250 ML EACH)

2.2 lbs	clementines (about 15)	1 kg
10 cups	water	2.4 L
5 cups	granulated sugar	1 kg
6 tbsp	lemon juice	90 mL
1	vanilla bean, split and scraped	1
5 oz	white chocolate, chopped	150 g

TIPS

Choose a good white chocolate made with cocoa butter. I prefer Valrhona Ivoire.

Because of the white chocolate, this marmalade has a shorter shelf life than others and will only keep for about 1 year.

Cut off and discard the ends of the clementines, then quarter them lengthwise and slice them as thinly as possible, discarding any seeds. Place the slices in a large pot with the water, cover and let soak overnight (but not more than 24 hours).

The next day, uncover the pot and bring the clementine mixture to a boil over high heat. Reduce the heat and simmer, stirring occasionally, for 1 to 2 hours or until the peels are tender and most of the water has evaporated. Increase the heat to medium-high and stir in the sugar, lemon juice and vanilla bean. Bring to a boil, stirring often to dissolve the sugar.

Measure the white chocolate into a heatproof bowl that is large enough to hold the whole mixture, then pour in the clementine mélange. Wait about 30 seconds, then stir to melt the chocolate. Place a circle of parchment paper directly on the surface and refrigerate overnight.

The next day, prepare the jars and lids.

Transfer the clementine mixture to a large pot or preserving pan and bring to a boil over medium-high heat, stirring often. Boil hard, stirring often, until the setting point is reached (see page 17). Remove from heat and let rest for 5 minutes, stirring occasionally. Remove the vanilla bean (see tip, page 20).

Ladle marmalade into the hot jars to within ¼ inch (0.5 cm) of the rim. Remove any air bubbles and wipe rims. Place the lids on the jars and screw the bands on until fingertip-tight. Process in a boiling water canner for 10 minutes.

CHRISTMAS CLEMENTINE MARMALADE

LITTLE ORANGES ARE SO UBIQUITOUS at Christmas that I assumed the variety on offer to be universal. Being a child of the West, that meant mandarin oranges to me. Imagine my delight when I discovered a new taste in my first Montreal winter! Here, we get clementines, which look almost identical to mandarins but are noticeably tangier, which works perfectly for marmalade-making. Of course, if you have mandarins, feel free to use them instead. This marmalade is assertively flavored with Christmas spices (and a nip of rum) to get you into the holiday spirit.

MAKES SIX OR SEVEN JARS (8 OZ/250 ML EACH)

2.5 lbs	clementines (about ½ a box)	1.15 kg
3 cups	granulated sugar	600 g
1¾ cups	packed brown sugar	400 g
½ tsp	Pie Spice (see box, below)	2 mL
⅔ cup	lemon juice	150 mL
2 tbsp	dark rum	30 mL

TIP

You could use pumpkin pie spice in place of the homemade Pie Spice, but I strongly suggest making your own. You can use it in pumpkin pie, apple pie — anywhere a fall or Christmas spice blend is called for.

Place the clementines in a large pot and add enough water so that they float freely. Cover and bring to a boil over high heat. Reduce the heat to medium and simmer for 1 to 2 hours or until soft.

In the meantime, prepare the jars and lids.

Drain the clementines, transfer them to a cutting board and let cool until you can handle them. Cut them into medium-fine pieces, discarding the stem end and any seeds.

In a large pot or preserving pan, combine the chopped clementines, granulated sugar, brown sugar, pie spice and lemon juice. Bring to a boil over medium-high heat, stirring often. Boil hard, stirring often, until the setting point is reached (see page 17). Remove from heat and let rest for 5 minutes, stirring occasionally. Stir in the rum.

Ladle marmalade into the hot jars to within ¼ inch (0.5 cm) of the rim. Remove any air bubbles and wipe rims. Place the lids on the jars and screw the bands on until fingertip-tight. Process in a boiling water canner for 10 minutes.

PIE SPICE

Using a clean coffee or spice grinder, grind together 6 allspice berries, 3 pieces of mace, 6 green cardamom pods, 1 whole star anise and 2 tsp (10 mL) whole cloves. Stir in 4 tsp (20 mL) ground cinnamon, 1½ tsp (7 mL) ground ginger and 1 tsp (5 mL) ground nutmeg. Makes about 3 tbsp (45 mL).

ARISTOCRAT'S MARMALADE

THIS MARMALADE IS FIT FOR A KING. It has that robust Seville flavor, tempered by creamy, rich milk chocolate, complemented by crunchy, fragrant toasted almonds and rounded out with a pinch of fleur de sel and a little hit of Scotch. While it's best consumed in a limo, horse-drawn carriage or four-poster bed, it's also excellent in the Marmalade Pecan Pie on page 174 (particularly the cocoa nib variation).

MAKES ABOUT SIX JARS (8 OZ/250 ML EACH)

2.2 lbs	Seville oranges (about 6)	1 kg
5 cups	granulated sugar	1 kg
½ cup	lemon juice	125 mL
7 oz	milk chocolate pistoles (preferably Valrhona Jivara)	200 g
3½ oz	toasted sliced almonds (see tip, at right)	100 g
¼ tsp	fleur de sel	1 mL
2 tbsp	Scotch or brandy	30 mL

Place the oranges in a large pot and add enough water so that they float freely. Cover and bring to a boil over high heat. Reduce the heat to medium and simmer until very soft, about 2 hours.

In the meantime, prepare the jars and lids.

Drain the oranges, transfer them to a cutting board and let cool until you can handle them. Cut them in half and discard the stem end and seeds. Slice the oranges into short strips.

In a large pot or preserving pan, combine the sliced oranges, sugar and lemon juice. Bring to a boil over medium-high heat, stirring often. Stir in the chocolate and almonds. Boil hard, stirring often, until the setting point is reached (see page 17).

Remove from heat and let rest for 5 minutes, stirring occasionally. Stir in the fleur de sel and Scotch.

Ladle marmalade into the hot jars to within ¼ inch (0.5 cm) of the rim. Remove any air bubbles and wipe rims. Place the lids on the jars and screw the bands on until fingertip-tight. Process in a boiling water canner for 10 minutes.

TIPS

Because this recipe uses whole oranges, it is better to have slightly more than the weight called for than it is to have slightly less. Use the number of oranges that allows you to meet or slightly exceed 2.2 lbs (1 kg).

To toast sliced almonds, spread them out on a baking sheet and toast in a 350°F (180°C) oven for 8 to 10 minutes, stirring occasionally, until golden and fragrant.

For a dairy-free marmalade, feel free to substitute dark chocolate, but pick one that's not too bitter.

If you'd like to make the marmalade without nuts, an equal weight of cocoa nibs is a fantastic substitute.

Because of the chocolate and nuts, this marmalade has a shorter shelf life than others and will keep only for about 1 year.

MARMGARITA

NO, THAT'S NOT A SPELLING ERROR: it's the name I chose for this marmalade based on the classic cocktail. At the time, it made me laugh. Whatever you think of the name, this lime preserve is sure to win you over. It is tender, sweet, salty, sour and a little bit boozy — a true revelation. It's so good that a group of six taking a marmalade workshop ate an entire pint jar during a tasting. Electrify your morning toast, use it to glaze a cheesecake or just eat it with a spoon the way most of us do ...

The citric acid restores the punchy acidity that the limes lose when they are boiled. It's fairly easy to find at grocery stores or at the pharmacy, sometimes sold as "sour salt."

MAKES ABOUT FIVE JARS (8 OZ/250 ML EACH)

1.1 lbs	limes (about 5)	500 g
2.7 oz	Seville orange or grapefruit (about ½)	75 g
5 cups	water	1.25 L
4⅓ cups	granulated sugar	875 g
¼ cup	lime juice	60 mL
1 tsp	coarse salt	5 mL
½ tsp	citric acid	2 mL
2 tbsp	silver tequila	30 mL
1 tbsp	triple sec	15 mL

Cut off and discard the ends of the limes and orange, then quarter them lengthwise and slice them as thinly as possible, discarding any seeds. Place the slices in a large pot with the water, cover and let soak overnight (but not more than 24 hours).

The next day, uncover the pot and bring the lime mixture to a boil over high heat. Reduce the heat and simmer, stirring occasionally, until the peels are tender and most of the water has evaporated, about 2 hours.

In the meantime, prepare the jars and lids.

Add the sugar, lime juice and salt to the pot, then increase the heat to medium-high and bring to a boil, stirring often. Boil hard, stirring often, until the setting point is reached (see page 17). Remove from heat and stir in the citric acid. Let rest for 5 minutes, stirring occasionally. Stir in the tequila and triple sec.

Ladle marmalade into the hot jars to within ¼ inch (0.5 cm) of the rim. Remove any air bubbles and wipe rims. Place the lids on the jars and screw the bands on until fingertip-tight. Process in a boiling water canner for 10 minutes.

BITTERS BLOOD ORANGE MARMALADE

BITTER HAS ALWAYS BEEN one of my favorite flavors, hence my abiding love of marmalade. I also love cocktail bitters and digestive bitters like Campari and Fernet. Here is where the two come together. Blood oranges make a gorgeous red marmalade, and their bitterness is enhanced by the addition of cocktail bitters.

MAKES ABOUT SIX JARS (8 OZ/250 ML EACH)

1.9 lbs	blood oranges (5 to 6 medium)	875 g
8 cups	water	1.9 L
6¼ cups	granulated sugar	1.25 kg
⅓ cup	lemon juice	75 mL
1½ tsp	bitters (preferably orange)	7 mL

Cut off and discard the ends of the oranges, then quarter them lengthwise and slice them as thinly as possible, discarding any seeds. Place the slices in a large pot with the water, cover and let soak overnight (but not more than 24 hours).

The next day, uncover the pot and bring the orange mixture to a boil over high heat. Reduce the heat and simmer, stirring occasionally, until the peels are tender and most of the water has evaporated, about 1 hour.

In the meantime, prepare the jars and lids.

Add the sugar and lemon juice to the pot, then increase the heat to medium-high and bring to a boil, stirring often. Boil hard, stirring often, until the setting point is reached (see page 17). Remove from heat and let rest for 5 minutes, stirring occasionally. Stir in the bitters.

Ladle marmalade into the hot jars to within ¼ inch (0.5 cm) of the rim. Remove any air bubbles and wipe rims. Place the lids on the jars and screw the bands on until fingertip-tight. Process in a boiling water canner for 10 minutes.

KEY LIME AND GINGER MARMALADE

KEY LIMES ARE A PAIN IN THE BUTT to work with, but their cuteness and fragrance make up for it. Just put on a good music mix or an audiobook and get to it. Substitute regular limes, if you wish.

MAKES ABOUT FOUR JARS (8 OZ/250 ML EACH)		
1.1 lbs	key limes (about 30)	500 g
5 cups	water	1.25 mL
4 cups + 2 tbsp	granulated sugar	825 g
3 tbsp	grated gingerroot	45 mL
1 tsp	ground ginger	5 mL
¼ cup	key lime juice	60 mL

> ## TIP
> To grate the gingerroot, peel it first then use a Japanese ceramic ginger grater or Microplane-style grater.

Cut off and discard the ends of the limes, then quarter them lengthwise and slice them as thinly as possible, discarding any seeds. Place the slices in a large pot with the water, cover and let soak overnight (but not more than 24 hours).

The next day, uncover the pot and bring the lime mixture to a boil over high heat. Reduce the heat and simmer, stirring occasionally, until the peels are tender and most of the water has evaporated, about 1 hour.

In the meantime, prepare the jars and lids.

Add the sugar, grated ginger, ground ginger and lime juice to the pot, then increase the heat to medium-high and bring to a boil, stirring often. Boil hard, stirring often, until the setting point is reached (see page 17). Remove from heat and let rest for 5 minutes, stirring occasionally.

Ladle marmalade into the hot jars to within ¼ inch (0.5 cm) of the rim. Remove any air bubbles and wipe rims. Place the lids on the jars and screw the bands on until fingertip-tight. Process in a boiling water canner for 10 minutes.

LEMON POPPY SEED MARMALADE

I THOUGHT IT WAS ABOUT TIME to bring the classic muffin flavor to the jam jar. The pale jelly spotted with black poppy seeds and slices of yellow peel looks very pretty.

MAKES ABOUT SIX JARS (8 OZ/250 ML EACH)		
2.2 lbs	lemons (about 8)	1 kg
10 cups	water	2.4 L
7 cups	granulated sugar	1.4 kg
½ cup	poppy seeds	60 g

Cut off and discard the ends of the lemons, then quarter them lengthwise and slice them as thinly as possible, discarding any seeds. Place the slices in a large pot with the water, cover and let soak overnight (but not more than 24 hours).

The next day, uncover the pot and bring the lemon mixture to a boil over high heat. Reduce the heat and simmer, stirring occasionally, until the peels are tender and most of the water has evaporated, about 1 hour.

In the meantime, prepare the jars and lids.

Add the sugar and poppy seeds to the pot, then increase the heat to medium-high and bring to a boil, stirring often. Boil hard, stirring often, until the setting point is reached (see page 17). Remove from heat and let rest for 5 minutes, stirring occasionally.

Ladle marmalade into the hot jars to within ¼ inch (0.5 cm) of the rim. Remove any air bubbles and wipe rims. Place the lids on the jars and screw the bands on until fingertip-tight. Process in a boiling water canner for 10 minutes.

WHITE GRAPEFRUIT MARMALADE WITH VANILLA

I STOLE THIS IDEA from the ultra-talented chef Michelle Marek of the Société des Arts Technologique's Foodlab. The pairing is simple but totally genius. I found myself so lusting after its haunting floral flavor that I had to make it for myself. And now for you. Thanks, Michelle!

MAKES ABOUT FIVE JARS (8 OZ/250 ML EACH)

2.1 lbs	white grapefruit (about 3)	930 g
5 cups	granulated sugar	1 kg
6 tbsp	lemon juice	90 mL
1	vanilla bean, split and scraped	1

TIP

Because this recipe uses whole grapefruit, it is better to have slightly more than the weight called for than it is to have slightly less. Use the number of grapefruit that allows you to meet or slightly exceed 2.1 lbs (930 g).

Place the grapefruit in a large pot and add enough water so that they float freely. Cover and bring to a boil over high heat. Reduce the heat to medium and simmer for 1 to 2 hours or until very soft.

In the meantime, prepare the jars and lids.

Drain the grapefruit, transfer them to a cutting board and let cool until you can handle them. Cut them in half and discard the stem end and any seeds. Slice the grapefruit into strips about 2 inches (5 cm) long and ¼ inch (0.5 cm) thick.

In a large pot or preserving pan, combine the sliced grapefruit, sugar, lemon juice and vanilla bean. Bring to a boil over medium-high heat, stirring often. Boil hard, stirring often, until the setting point is reached (see page 17). Remove from heat and let rest for 5 minutes, stirring occasionally. Remove the vanilla bean (see tip, page 20).

Ladle marmalade into the hot jars to within ¼ inch (0.5 cm) of the rim. Remove any air bubbles and wipe rims. Place the lids on the jars and screw the bands on until fingertip-tight. Process in a boiling water canner for 10 minutes.

SWEET TEA MARMALADE

I GOT THE IDEA FOR THIS MARMALADE while visiting a friend in Atlanta, Georgia. I've always loved the ubiquity of iced tea in the South — simply called sweet or unsweet tea (I remember being very confused the first time it was offered to me at a diner in North Carolina). Iced tea is often served with lemons, so it was an obvious flavor choice to be transformed into marmalade. Serve it with buttermilk biscuits and you have a Southern version of scones and jam!

Use a regular old black tea like Red Rose or PG Tips for this. The sweet tea vodka is optional, but if you can get it, it's a nice little flavor booster.

MAKES ABOUT FIVE JARS (8 OZ/250 ML EACH)

- Jelly bag or sieve lined with a double layer of cheesecloth

2.3 lbs	lemons (about 9), divided	1.05 kg
10½ cups	water, divided	2.5 L
3	black tea bags, divided	3
5 cups + 2 tbsp	granulated sugar	1.025 kg
3 tbsp	lemon juice	45 mL
¼ cup	sweet tea vodka (optional)	60 mL

Cut 1.3 lbs (600 g) of the lemons (about 5) into eighths. Place them in a wide pot and add 6 cups (1.5 L) water. Cover and bring to a boil over high heat. Reduce the heat to medium and simmer until soft, about 1 hour.

Place 2 tea bags in a large bowl. Pour the lemon mixture through a damp jelly bag suspended over the bowl. Let the tea infuse while the lemons drip for 10 minutes, then remove and discard the tea bags. Let the lemons continue to drip overnight. Set the tea-infused lemon water aside and discard the solids from the bag.

Meanwhile, cut off and discard the ends of the remaining lemons, then quarter them lengthwise and slice them as thinly as possible, discarding any seeds. Place the slices in a large pot with the remaining water, cover and let soak overnight.

The next day, uncover the pot and bring the lemon mixture to a boil over high heat. Reduce the heat and simmer, stirring occasionally, until the peels are tender and most of the water has evaporated, about 1 hour.

In the meantime, prepare the jars and lids.

Add the tea-infused lemon water, the remaining tea bag, and the sugar and lemon juice to the pot, then increase the heat to medium-high and bring to a boil, stirring often. Boil hard, stirring often, until the setting point is reached (see page 17). Remove from heat and let rest for 5 minutes, stirring occasionally. Discard the tea bag. Stir in the sweet tea vodka (if using).

Ladle marmalade into the hot jars to within ¼ inch (0.5 cm) of the rim. Remove any air bubbles and wipe rims. Place the lids on the jars and screw the bands on until fingertip-tight. Process in a boiling water canner for 10 minutes.

THREE CITRUS MARMALADE

FEEL FREE TO MIX AND MATCH different kinds of citrus fruits, as long as the overall weight stays the same, at about 2 lbs (885 g). Minneolas and tangerines are particularly pleasing. Please do not use limes, however — boiling them whole results in tough, leathery skins, and you will be sad.

MAKES ABOUT FIVE JARS (8 OZ/250 ML EACH)

13 oz	oranges (about 2 large)	365 g
10 oz	grapefruit (about 1 medium)	280 g
8.5 oz	lemons (about 2)	240 g
4¾ cups	granulated sugar	950 g
6 tbsp	lemon juice	90 mL
½	vanilla bean, split and scraped (optional)	½

TIP

Because this recipe uses whole citrus fruits, it is better to have slightly more than the weight called for than it is to have slightly less. Use the number of fruit that allows you to meet or slightly exceed 13 oz (365 g) for the oranges, 10 oz (280 g) for the grapefruit and 8.5 oz (240 g) for the lemons.

Place the oranges, grapefruit and lemons in a large pot and add enough water so that they float freely. Cover and bring to a boil over high heat. Reduce the heat to medium and simmer until very soft, about 2 hours.

In the meantime, prepare the jars and lids.

Drain the citrus fruits, transfer them to a cutting board and let cool until you can handle them. Cut them in half and discard the stem end and seeds. Chop the fruits to desired thickness.

In a large pot or preserving pan, combine the sliced citrus fruits, sugar, lemon juice and vanilla bean (if using). Bring to a boil over medium-high heat, stirring often. Boil hard, stirring often, until the setting point is reached (see page 17). Remove from heat and let rest for 5 minutes, stirring occasionally. Remove the vanilla bean (if using).

Ladle marmalade into the hot jars to within ¼ inch (0.5 cm) of the rim. Remove any air bubbles and wipe rims. Place the lids on the jars and screw the bands on until fingertip-tight. Process in a boiling water canner for 10 minutes.

VARIATION

Three Citrus Ginger Marmalade: Add 1½ tbsp (22 mL) grated gingerroot and ½ tsp (2 mL) ground ginger with the sugar.

JELLIES AND BUTTERS

❧

JELLIES AND BUTTERS

JELLIES

The difference between a jelly and a jam is kind of like the difference between pulp-free and extra-pulp orange juice: one is smooth and the other is chunky. Whereas jams are a mixture of fruit and sugar, jellies are a mixture of fruit juice and sugar.

Jellies aren't really very à la mode. They seem mostly relegated to English tea parties of the past, or weird diners with dusty jam caddies. It makes sense that they're less prevalent in the artisanal preserving community, where commercial pectin is frowned upon — it can be hard to get a very jell-y jelly without it. Citrus fruits, currants, quince, cranberries and apples are among the fruits most suited to jelly because of their high pectin content, though I'm not above using commercial pectin occasionally. You will certainly notice that in this chapter's recipes.

I'm all for a jelly revival. For one thing, they're very beautiful: because there aren't any pieces of pesky fruit to get in the way, you're left with a crystal-clear preserve. Jars of jelly in the sunshine look like jewels. And though they're delicious spread on toast, they're also great for filling cookies, easy to melt down for glazing tarts and good for whisking into marinades.

You will need a jelly bag for most of these recipes if you're intent on getting a very clear, crystalline jelly. You can find them wherever canning supplies are sold. Mine's an old French one, basically just a big linen cloth. Make sure to dampen the jelly bag before use so it doesn't absorb your precious fruit juice. Wash your jelly bag after each use and hang it to dry, and it will last a very long time.

If you make a lot of jelly, you might want to invest in a steam juicer. It's a simple three-tiered contraption that uses water vapor to extract the juice from fruit. I felt like my life changed when I got mine! It makes extracting juice totally painless — just throw your fruit into the steamer basket and an hour or so later pour the juice off. No tedious coring or stemming necessary. Try to find one made of stainless steel, rather than aluminum, with the plastic tube placed high up, where there will be no chance of it melting or deforming near the heat of the burner.

Test a jelly for doneness just as you would a jam — with a teaspoon (5 mL) on a plate in the freezer for 2 minutes (see page 17 for more details). You're looking for a distinct wrinkle when you push it.

Jellies will keep for 1 year stored in a dark, cool place.

BUTTERS

A fruit butter is a fruit preserve that is so named because it resembles softened butter in its smooth spreadability — it rarely actually contains butter. To make a fruit butter, fruits are cooked with liquid until they are very soft, then puréed and cooked down until very thick. They are the absolute essence of concentrated fruit. Because of this, they also tend to contain less sugar than other spreads. I love their silky texture for sandwiching cookies or slathering on toast.

You will need a food processor or food mill to break your fruit down into a purée, though I suppose if you're feeling tough, you could also force it through a regular old sieve for a little exercise.

You'll notice in the instructions that butters are cooked a little differently than jams or jellies. Because they get so thick before they're done, you'll need to gradually reduce the heat to prevent the butter from burning. They also tend to spit and splatter more than other preserves, on account of their viscosity, so I recommend stirring often, and wearing an oven mitt if you're cooking a particularly lively batch!

The doneness test for a fruit butter is also a little different than for jams or jellies. There are a few ways to test for the setting point, but my favorite is to mound a teaspoon (5 mL) of the butter on a small plate. If it doesn't hold its shape at all, keep cooking it. If it holds its shape, that's a good sign, but now wait a few minutes and see whether a ring of clear liquid forms around the edges. If it does, that means there's still water in there that needs to be evaporated. When your butter is done, it will mound up on the plate and, after resting for a few minutes, it will have formed a wrinkly skin and should have only a barely perceptible ring of liquid around the edges.

SZARLOTKA JELLY

I WAS LUCKY ENOUGH TO GO to Poland with my band to play shows in Krakow and Warsaw. There I was introduced to a lovely cocktail called a *szarlotka*, made simply of Bison Grass Vodka mixed with unpasteurized apple juice. Honestly, it's a little too good — it's very easy to drink very many! I was inspired to make a jelly with the same flavors when I got some sweetgrass from Kamouraska, Quebec. It smells so incredible and goes so well with the apple. Feel free to omit the vodka — the sweetgrass is the star of the show here. You can find it at health food stores or herb shops.

MAKES ABOUT FOUR JARS (8 OZ/250 ML EACH)

3 cups	granulated sugar	600 g
¼ cup	powdered pectin	50 g
5	sweetgrass strands	5 g
4 cups	unsweetened apple cider or unfiltered juice (see tip, below)	1 L
¼ cup	vodka (preferably Bison Grass Vodka)	60 mL

Prepare the jars and lids.

In a large pot or preserving pan, combine the sugar, pectin, sweetgrass and apple juice. Bring to a boil over medium-high heat, stirring often. Boil hard, stirring often, for 1 minute. Remove from heat and let rest for 5 minutes, stirring occasionally. Stir in the vodka.

Ladle jelly into the hot jars to within ¼ inch (0.5 cm) of the rim. Remove any air bubbles and wipe rims. Place the lids on the jars and screw the bands on until fingertip-tight. Process in a boiling water canner for 10 minutes.

> ### TIPS
>
> Be sure to use a nonalcoholic (called "sweet" or "soft") cider for this jelly, and make sure there is no sugar added. Look for apple cider or unfiltered apple juice at farmers' markets, farm stands, some supermarkets and health food stores.
>
> Bison Grass Vodka is flavored with sweetgrass.

SUSIE'S APPLE BOURBON TODDY JELLY

NOT ONLY DOES MY AUNT SUSIE have a sour cherry tree (see page 70), she also has an apple tree. She invented this delectable recipe to use up her abundance of apples, but it's also worth going out and buying some to make it. She recommends using a combination of apples, or else a sweet-tart variety like Pink Lady. As for the bourbon, she uses Maker's Mark, but there are a number of reputable brands on the market — my favorite is Bulleit. On a cold winter's night you can stir a few spoonfuls of this jelly into a mug of hot water for a restorative drink.

MAKES ABOUT FIVE JARS (8 OZ/250 ML EACH)

- Jelly bag

4.4 lbs	apples (12 to 13)	2 kg
½ tsp	ground cinnamon	2 mL
¼ tsp	ground cloves	1 mL
¼ tsp	freshly grated nutmeg	1 mL
½ tsp	butter	2 mL
1	package (1.75 oz/49 g) Ball or Bernardin No Sugar Needed pectin	1
2 cups	granulated sugar	400 g
½ cup	bourbon	125 mL

Remove the stem and blossom ends from the apples, but don't peel or core. Coarsely chop the apples.

Place the chopped apples in a large pot with enough water to cover (about 4 to 5 cups/1 to 1.25 L). Bring to a boil over high heat, stirring often. Reduce the heat to medium-low, cover, leaving the lid ajar, and cook, stirring and crushing the apples occasionally, until softened. This should take about 20 minutes — you want to stop cooking before it turns into applesauce!

Pour the apple mixture through a damp jelly bag suspended over a large bowl and let drip, without squeezing, for several hours or overnight.

In the meantime, prepare the jars and lids.

Measure 4 cups (1 L) apple juice into a large pot. (If you don't have enough apple juice, add enough water to make up the difference.) Stir in the cinnamon, cloves, nutmeg and butter. Stir in the pectin until dissolved. Bring to a full rolling boil over medium-high heat, then add the sugar all at once. Stir to dissolve the sugar and return to a full rolling boil. Boil hard for 1 minute. Remove from heat and skim off any foam. Stir in the bourbon.

Ladle jelly into the hot jars to within ¼ inch (0.5 cm) of the rim. Remove any air bubbles and wipe rims. Place the lids on the jars and screw the bands on until fingertip-tight. Process in a boiling water canner for 10 minutes.

SEA BUCKTHORN JELLY

I FIRST ENCOUNTERED SEA BUCKTHORN berries at Pâtisserie Rhubarbe, where Stephanie Labelle uses them to make a compote and a fluid gel to garnish her amazing cheesecake. The little berries are bright orange and very sour — not very nice to eat raw. They're also nutrient-dense, boasting 15 times more vitamin C than oranges. High in pectin, these berries make a jelly that sets easily and is addictively sweet and tart.

MAKES ABOUT FIVE JARS (4 OZ/125 ML EACH)

- Jelly bag

2.2 lbs	fresh or frozen sea buckthorn berries (see tips, below)	1 kg
2 cups	water	500 mL
¾ to 1 cup	freshly squeezed orange juice	175 to 250 mL
2½ cups	granulated sugar	500 g

TIPS

Sea buckthorn berries are cultivated in Nevada, Arizona and several Canadian provinces. If you can't find them, you can also prepare this recipe using red currants.

If you don't have a kitchen scale, you'll need 8 cups (1.9 L) sea buckthorn berries (or 6 cups/1.5 L red currants) for this recipe.

In a large pot, combine the sea buckthorn berries and water. Bring to a boil over medium-high heat. Reduce the heat and simmer until the berries are quite soft and have fully relinquished their juice, about 20 minutes.

Pour the berry mixture through a damp jelly bag suspended over a large bowl and let drip, without squeezing, for several hours or overnight.

In the meantime, prepare the jars and lids.

Measure the berry juice (you should have about 1⅔ cups/400 mL) and add enough orange juice to make 2½ cups (625 mL). Stir the sugar into the juice, then transfer to a large pot or preserving pan. Bring to a full rolling boil over medium-high heat. Skim well, then continue to boil until the setting point is reached (see page 17). This should take less than 10 minutes, so stay close. Remove from heat and let rest for 5 minutes, stirring occasionally.

Ladle jelly into the hot jars to within ¼ inch (0.5 cm) of the rim. Remove any air bubbles and wipe rims. Place the lids on the jars and screw the bands on until fingertip-tight. Process in a boiling water canner for 10 minutes.

SUSIE'S SOUR CHERRY JELLY WITH VANILLA

HAVING A SOUR CHERRY TREE (and a backyard in which to keep it) is one of my true dreams and life goals. Fortunately, while I wait for that to materialize, my Aunt Susie acts as a generous benefactor when I visit Alberta, supplying me with bags full of frozen sour cherries from her tree, as well as this delicious jelly.

MAKES FIVE OR SIX JARS (8 OZ/250 ML EACH)

- Jelly bag

1.7 lbs	pitted sour cherries	750 g
½ cup	water	125 mL
1	vanilla bean, split	1
½ tsp	butter	2 mL
1	package (1.75 oz/49 g) Ball or Bernardin No Sugar Needed pectin	1
3 cups	granulated sugar	600 g
3 tbsp	kirsch (optional)	45 mL

TIP

If you don't have a kitchen scale, you'll need 5 cups (1.25 L) sour cherries for this recipe.

Place the cherries in a large stainless steel saucepan and crush them with your hands or a potato masher. (It's probably easier to do this in two batches: crush the first lot, then add the second and crush again.) Add the water and scrape the vanilla bean seeds into the pan. Bring to a boil over medium-high heat. Reduce the heat to medium-low, cover and simmer for about 10 minutes or until the cherries have given up all their juice.

Pour the cherry mixture through a damp jelly bag suspended over a large bowl and let drip, without squeezing, for several hours or overnight.

In the meantime, prepare the jars and lids.

Measure 4 cups (1 L) cherry juice into a large pot. (If you don't have enough cherry juice, add enough water to make up the difference.) Stir in the butter. Stir in the pectin until dissolved. Bring to a full rolling boil over medium-high heat, then add the sugar all at once. Stir to dissolve the sugar and return to a full rolling boil. Boil hard for 1 minute. Remove from heat and skim off any foam. Stir in the kirsch (if using).

Ladle jelly into the hot jars to within ¼ inch (0.5 cm) of the rim. Remove any air bubbles and wipe rims. Place the lids on the jars and screw the bands on until fingertip-tight. Process in a boiling water canner for 10 minutes.

PLUM RASPBERRY BUTTER WITH VANILLA BEAN

I FIRST MADE THIS FLAVOR AS A JAM for wedding favors, and was glad to find how well it translated to butter format. As much as I love raspberry seeds, this smooth spread is kind of magical because its flavor is hard to decipher. You just want to keep eating more to figure it out.

MAKES ABOUT THREE JARS (8 OZ/250 ML EACH)

• Food mill or food processor

2.2 lbs	plums (about 7 large)	1 kg
⅔ cup	water, divided	150 mL
8.8 oz	raspberries	250 g
3 cups	granulated sugar	600 g
3 tbsp	lemon juice	45 mL
1	vanilla bean, split and scraped	1

TIPS

If you don't have a kitchen scale, you'll need 2 cups (500 mL) raspberries for this recipe.

Don't throw out the vanilla bean after removing it from the fruit butter! It still has lots of flavor. Rinse it and then leave it to dry out completely in a warm place (like on top of the oven), then tuck it into granulated sugar to make vanilla sugar, or save up a bunch and use them to infuse rum or vodka for homemade vanilla extract.

Pit and coarsely chop the plums. You should have about 7 cups (1.75 L).

In a pot, combine the plums and ½ cup (125 mL) water. Cover and bring to a boil over high heat. Reduce the heat to medium and cook, stirring occasionally, for about 30 minutes or until the plums are very soft and have begun to break down.

In the meantime, prepare the jars and lids.

Press the plum mixture through a food mill, discarding skins, or purée it in a food processor. Transfer the plum purée to a large pot or preserving pan.

In a smaller pot, combine the raspberries and the remaining water. Bring to a boil over medium heat, stirring often. Cover and simmer over medium heat, stirring occasionally, for about 15 minutes or until the raspberries are very soft — almost a sauce. Force the raspberry mixture through a strainer fine enough to remove the seeds. Add the raspberry pulp to the plum purée.

Add the sugar, lemon juice and vanilla bean to the plum-raspberry mixture. Bring to a boil over medium-high heat, stirring often. Boil, stirring often and gradually reducing the heat, until the setting point is reached (see page 17). Remove the vanilla bean (see tip, at left).

Ladle butter into the hot jars to within ¼ inch (0.5 cm) of the rim. Remove any air bubbles and wipe rims. Place the lids on the jars and screw the bands on until fingertip-tight. Process in a boiling water canner for 10 minutes.

APRICOT BUTTER

I COULD GO ON AND ON about how glorious this butter is. Apricots are one of my very favorite fruits, and there's something about them in this silky guise that's extra-special.

MAKES ABOUT SIX JARS (8 OZ/250 ML EACH)

- Immersion blender, food mill, food processor or blender

4.4 lbs	apricots (about 50 small)	2 kg
1 cup	apricot nectar	250 mL
6 tbsp	lemon juice	90 mL
4 cups	granulated sugar	800 g

Pit and quarter the apricots. You should have about 13 cups (3 L).

In a large pot, combine the apricots, apricot nectar and lemon juice. Cover and bring to a boil over medium-high heat. Reduce the heat to medium and cook, stirring occasionally, for about 30 minutes or until the apricots are very soft and have begun to break down.

In the meantime, prepare the jars and lids.

Remove the apricot mixture from the heat and let cool for a few minutes before puréeing. You can do this with an immersion blender, a food mill, a food processor or a blender. Just don't overdo it — you don't want the apricots completely liquefied.

In a large pot or preserving pan, combine the apricot purée and sugar. Bring to a boil over medium-high heat, stirring often. Boil, stirring often and gradually reducing the heat, until the setting point is reached (see page 17).

Ladle butter into the hot jars to within ¼ inch (0.5 cm) of the rim. Remove any air bubbles and wipe rims. Place the lids on the jars and screw the bands on until fingertip-tight. Process in a boiling water canner for 10 minutes.

VARIATION

If tonka bean is available, add 1½ tsp (7 mL) grated tonka bean (about 1) with the sugar. With a flavor that has always made me think fondly of vanilla café au lait, the tonka bean, a dried legume from South America, is very much worth seeking out. The trouble is, as of this book's publication, tonka bean is banned by the FDA because it contains coumarin, which the FDA considers a drug. But if you're making this butter outside of the U.S., or if the ban is lifted by the time you're preparing this recipe, try adding the grated tonka bean — it's incredibly good.

> **TIP**
>
> If using fresh lemon juice, you'll need about 2 lemons for 6 tbsp (90 mL) lemon juice.

BROWN BUTTER APPLE BUTTER

I'VE ALWAYS HAD RESPECT for apple butter, but it's never been the first — or even the fourth — preserve I'd reach for when looking to fancy up my toast. It can be a bit of a wallflower, and frankly I think it's because most apple butters don't really let the fruit shine. Apples have become so associated with cinnamon that you could add the spice to Ritz crackers or turnips, tell people they're eating apples, and they'll swallow it no questions asked. I prefer instead to round out the delicious flavor of apple with brown butter, one of my favorite flavors. The result could almost be mistaken for caramel sauce. Try it in crepes, on oatmeal or sandwiched between the brown butter cookies on page 177. Just be sure to use an apple with a lot of flavor, and one that will break down easily during cooking. Cortlands are my favorite.

MAKES ABOUT FIVE JARS (8 OZ/250 ML EACH)

- Food processor

4.4 lbs	apples (about 10 large), peeled, quartered and cored	2 kg
2 cups	apple cider	500 mL
3 tbsp	lemon juice	45 mL
7 tbsp	unsalted butter	100 g
2 cups	granulated sugar	400 g

In a large pot, combine the apples, apple cider and lemon juice. Cover and bring to a boil over high heat. Reduce the heat to medium and simmer, stirring occasionally, for about 30 minutes or until the apples are very soft.

In the meantime, prepare the jars and lids.

Meanwhile, in a small saucepan, cook the butter over medium heat until it turns golden and smells very nutty and toffee-like. Immediately pour the butter into the bowl of a food processor.

When the apples are ready, add the apple mixture to the food processor with the brown butter and purée until smooth and emulsified. Move on to the next step quickly so that the apple purée stays hot.

Caramelize the sugar in the same large pot or a preserving pan in which you will cook the jam. I like to make a dry caramel — put enough sugar into the pot to cover the bottom and heat on medium-high. Don't stir it! Just wait for the sugar to caramelize by itself, then stir in a few more tablespoons (45 to 60 mL). Once this has dissolved and caramelized, add some more.

When all the sugar has been transformed into caramel, remove the pot from the heat and immediately add the hot apple purée. Be careful — it may splatter. Stir well, then return to the heat. Boil, stirring often and gradually reducing the heat, until the setting point is reached (see page 17).

Ladle butter into the hot jars to within ¼ inch (0.5 cm) of the rim. Remove any air bubbles and wipe rims. Place the lids on the jars and screw the bands on until fingertip-tight. Process in a boiling water canner for 10 minutes.

TIPS

It is unusual to include butter in home canning recipes, but this recipe has been safety-tested to ensure the correct pH and processing time. Do not attempt to use fats or animal products in other recipes that have not been tested. For food safety, this recipe must be prepared exactly as written, with no changes to the measurements. Be sure to measure accurately.

Store this apple butter in a cool, dark place with little temperature fluctuation for 3 to 4 months. Alternatively, for greater assurance of freshness, store it in the refrigerator.

CANNED FRUITS

❧

CANNED FRUITS

Canning fruit became kind of obsolete for a lot of people with the advent of commercial canneries, but if you grow fruit or want to eat local foods throughout the winter, canning fruit is a great solution. Besides, canning your own fruits allows you to play with flavors and invent combinations you could never find on the supermarket shelf. Canned fruit is basically dessert in a jar!

You can preserve fruit whole, halved or chopped. Many fruits will need to be peeled, too. Treat fruits that oxidize easily with an acidic solution to prevent browning — keep them in lemon water (about 3 tbsp/45 mL lemon juice for every 4 cups/1 L water), for instance, until you're ready to use them.

Most fruit can be canned even just in water, but to preserve color and texture, canning in syrup is preferable. Syrup can be anywhere from light to extra-heavy. I prefer a light to medium syrup for most fruit. Honey can be substituted for some of the sugar, and any type of flavoring can be used to perfume the syrup. Experiment with different herbs, spices, liquors and teas.

If you are canning a low-acid fruit, such as bananas, figs, melons or papaya, make sure your recipe calls for additional acid (such as lemon juice). As always, it is important to follow the heat processing times specified in the recipe.

Fruits are either raw- or hot-packed. Raw-packing fruits means that the fruits are packed fresh into the jars, perhaps cut or treated to prevent discoloration, but uncooked. Hot syrup is then poured over them. Hot-packing fruits involves cooking the fruit in the hot syrup before filling the jars. Why the two methods? Hot-packing fruit helps you get more in your jars and prevents flotation (the fruits will release some moisture when heated), but raw-packing will help keep the shape of fragile fruits such as raspberries or grapefruit segments. Either way, make sure to remove all the air bubbles you can from the jars.

Canned fruits will keep for 1 year in a cool, dark place, though generally they are better within 6 months, especially if they don't contain much sugar.

FIGS IN FERNET SYRUP

FERNET BRANCA IS A BITTER ITALIAN SPIRIT that's a bit of an acquired taste. If you don't like drinks that taste like they could be medicine, then it's probably not for you. People who love it, though, love it with a passion, and I count myself among them. You can substitute Chartreuse or even brandy, if you prefer, or you can leave the liquor out if you want to preserve the unadulterated taste of delicious black figs. Serve these over ice cream or baked in a frangipane tart.

MAKES ABOUT THREE JARS (1 PINT/500 ML EACH)

2¾ cups + 2 tbsp	granulated sugar	575 g
3 cups	water	750 mL
2.2 lbs	black figs, stems trimmed off and figs halved lengthwise	1 kg

PER JAR

3 tbsp	Fernet Branca	45 mL
1½ tsp	bottled lemon juice	7 mL

TIPS

If you don't have a kitchen scale, you'll need about 20 medium-size figs for this recipe.

Do not substitute freshly squeezed lemon juice in this recipe. While acidity varies from one lemon to another, bottled lemon juice has a constant pH and will ensure a safe pH level for these figs, which are a low-acid fruit.

In a large saucepan, combine the sugar and water. Bring to a boil over high heat, stirring to dissolve the sugar. Remove from heat and add the figs, cut side down. Let cool to room temperature, then cover and refrigerate overnight.

The next day, prepare the jars and lids.

Heat the figs in syrup over medium heat until heated through. If you feel you need to stir them, do so very gently to keep the fragile figs intact.

Add Fernet and lemon juice to each hot jar. Using a slotted spoon, transfer figs to the jars, packing them in gently to within a generous ½ inch (1 cm) of the rim. Pour in hot syrup to within ½ inch (1 cm) of the rim. Remove any air bubbles, add more syrup if necessary and wipe rims. Place the lids on the jars and screw the bands on until fingertip-tight. Process in a boiling water canner for 45 minutes.

Allow a few weeks for the flavors to meld before opening.

RASPBERRIES IN SYRUP

THIS WAS MY ABSOLUTE FAVORITE canned good as a child. I would beg my grandmother to bring up a large jar from the cellar every time I visited the farm. Even when I, a squeamish child, found a huge dead beetle in one jar, I was not put off. It is the one recipe I asked my grandmother to mail me when I started to can, and I still have the handwritten recipe card she sent. At the bottom, she simply wrote, "I remember how you liked them." I still do. And I framed that recipe card.

The addition of the vanilla bean is mine, and certainly isn't necessary.

MAKES ABOUT FIVE JARS (1 PINT/500 ML EACH)

3 cups + 2 tbsp	granulated sugar	625 g
5 cups	water	1.25 L
1	vanilla bean, split and scraped (optional)	1
2.7 lbs	raspberries	1.2 kg

TIP

If you don't have a kitchen scale, you'll need 10½ cups (2.5 L) raspberries for this recipe.

Prepare the jars and lids.

In a medium pot, combine the sugar, water and vanilla bean. Bring to a boil over high heat, stirring to dissolve the sugar.

Carefully pack raspberries into the hot jars to within a generous ½ inch (1 cm) of the rim. You want to get as many in as you can without crushing them. I like to put the vanilla bean in one of the jars as well. Pour in hot syrup to within ½ inch (1 cm) of the rim. Remove any air bubbles, add more syrup if necessary and wipe rims. Place the lids on the jars and screw the bands on until fingertip-tight. Process in a boiling water canner for 15 minutes.

POIRES BELLE HÉLÈNE

POIRES BELLE HÉLÈNE IS A FRENCH DESSERT created by the great chef Escoffier and named after a Jacques Offenbach opera. It consists of poached pears served with vanilla ice cream and sprinkled with crystallized violets, accompanied by a pitcher of hot chocolate sauce. This is my pantry version. Open up a jar for an instant dessert. I like to use Flemish Beauty pears, a variety cultivated in Quebec, but you can use any small, firm, fragrant pear. And use the best cocoa you can afford. The violet extract is optional, but it does lend a lovely floral note. You can find it online or at a cake decorating store.

MAKES ABOUT FIVE JARS (1 PINT/500 ML EACH)

4.9 lbs	pears (about 15 small)	2.2 kg
	Lemon water (see page 78) or citric acid water	
3¾ cups	granulated sugar	750 g
4 cups	water	1 L
3 tbsp	bottled lemon juice	45 mL
1 cup	unsweetened cocoa powder	110 g
⅛ tsp	salt	0.5 mL

PER JAR

1 tbsp	Poire Williams	15 mL
1 tbsp	bottled lemon juice	15 mL
¼ tsp	violet extract (optional)	1 mL

Prepare the jars and lids.

Peel, core and slice the pears lengthwise into eighths. As you do this, transfer the pear slices to a bowl of lemon or citric acid water to prevent them from browning.

In a large pot, combine the sugar, water and lemon juice. Bring to a boil over high heat, stirring to dissolve the sugar. Add the pears, reduce the heat and simmer until the pears are heated through. (You can also do this step in batches, especially if the pears are quite ripe and there is a risk of overcooking.) Using a slotted spoon, transfer the pears to a large bowl.

Whisk the cocoa and salt into the syrup remaining in the pot. Bring to a boil, whisking constantly. Careful — the cocoa will make it prone to boiling over! Remove from heat and pour the syrup over the pears.

Add Poire Williams, lemon juice and violet extract (if using) to each hot jar. Using a slotted spoon, transfer pears to the jars, packing them in gently to within a generous ½ inch (1 cm) of the rim. Pour in hot syrup to within ½ inch (1 cm) of the rim. Remove any air bubbles, add more syrup if necessary and wipe rims. Place the lids on the jars and screw the bands on until fingertip-tight. Process in a boiling water canner for 25 minutes.

SCARLET PEARS

THESE PEARS TURN A BEAUTIFUL REDDISH-PINK from the red currant syrup. Open up a jar and you have instant poached pears to bake into a tart or serve over pound cake. Don't forget to save the syrup!

MAKES ABOUT FOUR JARS (1 PINT/500 ML EACH)

4 lbs	pears (about 12 small)	1.8 kg
	Lemon water (see page 78) or citric acid water	
1	batch (or 4 jars) Red Currant Syrup (page 98)	1

PER JAR

2 tbsp	crème de cassis	30 mL

TIP

Try to use just ripe pears: too ripe and they'll fall apart; underripe and they won't have a uniform texture. As always, my favorite variety is Flemish Beauty.

Prepare the jars and lids.

Peel, core and slice the pears lengthwise into eighths. As you do this, transfer the pear slices to a bowl of lemon or citric acid water to prevent them from browning.

In a large pot, bring the syrup to a boil over high heat. Add the pears, reduce the heat and simmer until the pears are heated through. (You can also do this step in batches, especially if the pears are quite ripe and there is a risk of overcooking.)

Add crème de cassis to each hot jar. Using a slotted spoon, transfer pears to the jars, packing them in gently to within a generous ½ inch (1 cm) of the rim. Pour in hot syrup to within ½ inch (1 cm) of the rim. Remove any air bubbles, add more syrup if necessary and wipe rims. Place the lids on the jars and screw the bands on until fingertip-tight. Process in a boiling water canner for 20 minutes.

APPLE COMPOTE, RHUBARBE-STYLE

THIS RECIPE COMES COURTESY OF STEPHANIE LABELLE, my old chum from pastry school who went on to open one of Montreal's best pastry shops, Pâtisserie Rhubarbe. Given how delicious this compote is, it's shockingly simple. There is genius in simplicity. I like to use Cortland apples, but any sweet-tart variety will work.

MAKES ABOUT SIX JARS (1 PINT/500 ML EACH)		
8.8 lbs	apples (about 18 medium)	4 kg
¾ cup	lemon juice	175 mL
¼ cup	olive oil	60 mL
1	vanilla bean, split and scraped	1
1¼ cups	granulated sugar	250 g

TIPS

If using fresh lemon juice, you'll need about 4 lemons for ¾ cup (175 mL) lemon juice.

It is unusual to include oil in home canning recipes, but this recipe has been safety-tested to ensure the correct pH and processing time. Do not attempt to use fats or animal products in other recipes that have not been tested. For food safety, this recipe must be prepared exactly as written, with no changes to the measurements. Be sure to measure accurately.

Store this compote in a cool, dark place with little temperature fluctuation. Alternatively, for greater assurance of freshness, store it in the refrigerator.

Prepare the jars and lids.

Peel, core and cut the apples into ½-inch (1 cm) cubes, then weigh out 6.6 lbs (3 kg). As you do this, transfer the apple cubes to a bowl and toss them with the lemon juice to prevent browning.

In a large pot, heat the olive oil and vanilla bean over medium heat. Add the apples and sugar. Cook, stirring often, until you have a mixture of sauce and soft pieces of apple. You are looking for a very chunky compote. This will take about 25 minutes. Remove from heat and remove the vanilla bean (see tip, page 71).

Ladle compote into the hot jars to within ½ inch (1 cm) of the rim. Remove any air bubbles and wipe rims. Place the lids on the jars and screw the bands on until fingertip-tight. Process in a boiling water canner for 20 minutes.

PEACH MELBA

ROSY, FRAGRANT PEACH HALVES in a syrup made of raspberries and vanilla bean. Need I say more? Likely not, but it seems of interest to note that this is the second preserve in the Preservation Society line inspired by a dessert created by the late, great Escoffier. (In pastry school I made myself a T-shirt that read "I ♡ Escoffier" and would wear it under my whites sometimes. What a nerd.)

These can be gently heated and served over ice cream, puréed for a peerless Bellini or served chilled and unadorned. Treat yourself.

MAKES ABOUT SIX JARS (1 PINT/500 ML EACH)

3 cups	granulated sugar	600 g
3⅔ cups	water	900 mL
1	vanilla bean, split and scraped	1
1.3 lbs	raspberries	600 g
4.4 lbs	peaches (about 16 small)	2 kg

In a large pot, combine the sugar, water and vanilla bean. Bring to a boil over high heat, stirring to dissolve the sugar. Add the raspberries, reduce the heat and simmer for 10 minutes or until the berries break down. Transfer the mixture to a fine-mesh sieve or a damp jelly bag set over a deep container and let drip overnight. Discard the solids.

The next day, prepare the jars and lids.

If you are picky about skins, you can peel the peaches. I don't bother with this step — I don't mind the skins, and they usually come off by themselves anyway when the peaches are heated in the syrup. But, if you're worried about it, boil a large pot of water and prepare a big bowl of ice water. Cut an X in the bottom of each peach. Plunge the peaches into the boiling water for 1 minute (not more), then use a slotted spoon to transfer them to the ice water. The skins should slide right off.

Skinned or not, halve the peaches lengthwise and remove the stones.

Transfer the raspberry syrup to a large pot and bring to a simmer over medium heat. Warm the peaches in the syrup, placing peaches in a single layer in the bottom of the pot (you will have to do this in a few batches).

Using a slotted spoon, transfer peaches to the hot jars, packing them in gently to within a generous ½ inch (1 cm) of the rim. Pour in hot syrup to within ½ inch (1 cm) of the rim. Remove any air bubbles, add more syrup if necessary and wipe rims. Place the lids on the jars and screw the bands on until fingertip-tight. Process in a boiling water canner for 25 minutes.

TIP
If you don't have a kitchen scale, you'll need 5 cups (1.25 L) raspberries for this recipe.

PLUMS IN SYRUP

MONT-ROYAL PLUMS ARE A VARIETY SPECIFIC to Quebec. They are cute and tiny and perfect for canning whole. I don't mind the seeds, but you can remove them if you like. Just don't forget to warn people if you do keep them. These are good with yogurt or ice cream, or on pound cake. Any leftover plum syrup makes a nice cocktail mixed with brandy and lemon juice. If you like, add a few vanilla beans to the syrup, or a handful of fresh lemon thyme or basil.

MAKES ABOUT SIX JARS (1 PINT/500 ML EACH)

4 lbs	Mont-Royal plums (see tip, below)	1.8 kg
3¼ cups	granulated sugar	650 g
5 cups	water	1.25 L

TIP

If you can't find Mont-Royal plums, use another small variety, like Mirabelles or Greengages, or halve or quarter and pit larger plums, such as Italian or Santa Rosa.

Prepare the jars and lids.

Stem the plums and cut an X in the bottom of each, to prevent them from bursting.

In a medium saucepan, combine the sugar and water. Bring to a boil over high heat, stirring to dissolve the sugar.

Carefully pack the plums into the hot jars to within a generous ½ inch (1 cm) of the rim. You want to pack them as snugly as possible without bruising them. Pour in hot syrup to within ½ inch (1 cm) of the rim. Remove any air bubbles, add more syrup if necessary and wipe rims. Place the lids on the jars and screw the bands on until fingertip-tight. Process in a boiling water canner for 20 minutes.

PRESERVATION SOCIETY FRUIT COCKTAIL

FRUIT COCKTAIL IS SUCH A BEAUTIFUL IDEA — almost dessert in a jar — but the version we all grew up on is pretty sad. One summer, walking through the market to choose fruit for the evening's canning class, I was overwhelmed by choice and decided to make my own version. Open a jar, divide the fruit among bowls and top with whipped cream or mascarpone — dessert is served! Though, if you have more time, a pound cake base to soak up the syrup couldn't hurt ...

MAKES ABOUT FOUR JARS (1 PINT/500 ML EACH)

5 oz	candied peel (see tip, below)	140 g
1.8 lbs	small apricots (about 20)	800 g
9 oz	cherries (see tips, below)	250 g
1½ cups	granulated sugar	300 g
3 cups	water	750 mL
1	vanilla bean, split and scraped	1

PER JAR

1 to 2 tbsp	brandy (optional)	15 to 30 mL

TIPS

Any kind of candied citrus peel will do to stuff the apricots, but I like homemade Seville orange or pink grapefruit peel best. See my Candied Peel recipe on page 146.

If you don't have a kitchen scale, you'll need 2 cups (500 mL) cherries for this recipe.

You may use sour or sweet cherries, though I tend to prefer the sour.

If you have it on hand, substitute apricot or cherry brandy (or both!) for extra flavor.

Prepare the jars and lids.

Cut the candied peel into 1- to 1½-inch (2.5 to 4 cm) pieces. You should have ½ cup (125 mL). Carefully pit each apricot by cutting a slit down the seam and removing the pit without cutting the apricot in half. Stuff one piece of candied peel into each apricot where the pit lived just a moment ago. (If you like, you can crack the pits with a hammer to extract the almonds — put a few in each jar to impart a subtle marzipan perfume.)

Trim or stem the cherries if you like and cut a small X in the bottom of each, to prevent them from bursting (leave the pits in).

In a medium saucepan, combine the sugar, water and vanilla bean. Bring to a boil over high heat, stirring to dissolve the sugar. Keep hot.

Pack the stuffed apricots and the cherries artfully into the hot jars, to within a generous ½ inch (1 cm) of the rim. If desired, add brandy to each jar.

Pour the hot syrup over the fruit to within ½ inch (1 cm) of the rim. I like to put the vanilla bean in one of the jars as well. Remove any air bubbles, add more syrup if necessary and wipe rims. Place the lids on the jars and screw the bands on until fingertip-tight. Process in a boiling water canner for 25 minutes.

NEW OLD-FASHIONED ORANGES

THESE ORANGE SLICES ARE PERHAPS EVEN MORE ATTRACTIVE than they are delicious, which is saying a lot. They would thus make an impressive gift. Copy the recipe for the New Old-Fashioned (page 159) onto a gift tag and attach it to the jar with ribbon. If you're not a cocktail person, they're also a great topping (underneathing?) for an upside-down cake, or a beautiful addition to an almond tart or a panna cotta. You will have some syrup left over, which is great mixed with seltzer water.

MAKES ABOUT SIX JARS (8 OZ/250 ML EACH)

2.6 lbs	small blood oranges (about 11)	1.175 kg
7½ cups	granulated sugar	1.5 kg

PER JAR

1½ tbsp	Aperol (see tip, below)	22 mL
1½ tsp	lemon juice	7 mL

> **TIP**
>
> If you can't find Aperol, use bourbon and a few dashes of bitters instead.

Carefully slice the oranges into ¼-inch (0.5 cm) rounds. Place them in a large pot, cover with water and bring to a boil over medium-high heat. Drain and repeat the blanching process. The goal here is to keep the slices — peel, flesh, membrane and all — intact for maximum beauty.

In a large pot, combine the sugar and 6 cups (1.5 L) water. Bring to a boil over high heat, stirring to dissolve the sugar. Gently add the orange slices, reduce the heat and simmer gently, gradually reducing the heat further, for 1 to 2 hours or until the oranges are translucent and the syrup has reduced significantly.

In the meantime, prepare the jars and lids.

Add Aperol and lemon juice to each hot jar. Using a slotted spoon, transfer orange slices to the jars, packing them in gently to within a generous ½ inch (1 cm) of the rim. Pour in hot syrup to within ½ inch (1 cm) of the rim. Remove any air bubbles, add more syrup if necessary and wipe rims. Place the lids on the jars and screw the bands on until fingertip-tight. Process in a boiling water canner for 15 minutes.

DANDY GRAPEFRUIT

I CREATED THIS RECIPE FOR SOMEONE I'm very sweet on — it's a combination of three of their favorite things: pink grapefruit, honey and tea. The whole, however, is larger than the sum of its parts. Somehow the flavor is reminiscent of lychee. I like to eat these plain, and well chilled.

MAKES ABOUT FOUR JARS (1 PINT/500 ML EACH)

8.8 lbs	pink grapefruit (about 12 medium)	4 kg
½ cup	granulated sugar	100 g
6 oz	honey	180 g
1 tbsp	black tea	5 g

TIP

For the tea, I use Monk's Blend, a very fruity black tea, but use any tea you like, or replace it altogether with fresh mint.

Prepare the jars and lids.

Segment each grapefruit by cutting off the top and bottom, then cutting away the peel and white pith, being careful not to remove too much fruit. Holding the naked grapefruit over a bowl to catch the juice, use a paring knife to slice between the membranes, freeing the segments.

Measure the reserved grapefruit juice. If you have less than 3 cups (750 mL), top it up with water. Transfer the juice to a medium pot and add the sugar and honey. Bring to a boil over high heat, stirring to dissolve the sugar. Remove from heat and add the tea. Let steep for 5 minutes, then strain.

Transfer the grapefruit segments to the hot jars, packing them in gently to within a generous ½ inch (1 cm) of the rim. Pour the hot syrup over the grapefruit to within ½ inch (1 cm) of the rim. Remove any air bubbles, add more syrup if necessary and wipe rims. Place the lids on the jars and screw the bands on until fingertip-tight. Process in a boiling water canner for 10 minutes.

SYRUPS

❦

SYRUPS

If only for the joy of mixing them with seltzer, I recommend making your own syrups. The result is better than most sodas I've had. But a syrup has more tricks up its sleeve than that: it can open up a whole new world of cocktails, jazz up a plain fruit salad, sweeten iced tea — the list goes on.

One piece of equipment that is fairly indispensable to syrup-making is a fine-mesh sieve. They're fairly inexpensive and good for all sorts of tasks, so I suggest you get one if you don't already have one. Without one, you're going to end up with cloudy or even chunky syrup, although you could always improvise with a cheesecloth setup. Up to you, MacGyver. If you are really worried about sediment, which can sometimes appear even after a run through the sieve, let the syrup drip through a sieve lined with a damp coffee filter.

Syrups will keep for 1 year in a cool, dark place, though generally they are better within 6 months, especially if they don't contain much sugar.

CONCORD GRAPE SYRUP

EVERY YEAR I LOOK FORWARD to the arrival of these dark-skinned grapes and eat as many as possible while they're in season (hey, grapes are supposed to be antiviral). I think they're best preserved in syrup form, the essence of grape. This syrup contains no water and just a pinch of citric acid to balance the sugar. Add it to soda water for the best grape soda ever, or add it to cocktails for mixological flair.

MAKES ABOUT SEVEN JARS (8 OZ/250 ML EACH)

6.6 lbs	Concord grapes, stemmed	3 kg
5 cups	granulated sugar	1 kg
¾ tsp	citric acid	3 mL

TIPS

If you don't have a kitchen scale, you'll need 18 cups (4.2 L) Concord grapes for this recipe.

If you own a steam juicer, this recipe is so easy! Just throw all the grapes into the steamer basket. When they have given up all their juice, decant it directly into a pot with the sugar and citric acid, and stir gently to dissolve!

Prepare the jars and lids.

In a large pot, combine the grapes and sugar, mashing them lightly to get the juices flowing. Bring to a gentle simmer over medium heat, stirring to dissolve the sugar. Allow the mixture to just barely simmer for 15 to 20 minutes, stirring occasionally, until the fruit has released all of its juice.

Pour the grape mixture into a fine-mesh sieve set over a deep container. Press gently against the grapes to extract as much liquid as possible. Discard the solids. Stir the citric acid into the syrup.

Pour syrup into the hot jars to within ½ inch (1 cm) of the rim. Wipe rims. Place the lids on the jars and screw the bands on until fingertip-tight. Process in a boiling water canner for 10 minutes.

SOUR CHERRY LEMONADE CONCENTRATE

THIS SYRUP IS A BOON TO HAVE ON HAND in the pantry on a hot summer's day. If you're on your own, add a few tablespoons to a glass of ice water, then refrigerate the rest for the next time you get thirsty. If you're serving a crowd, pour the whole jar into a big pitcher and dilute to taste. For a grownups-only party, add gin or vodka for a very easy, very drinkable cocktail.

MAKES ABOUT THREE JARS (1 PINT/500 ML EACH)

1 lb	pitted sour cherries	450 g
3 cups	granulated sugar	600 g
Pinch	salt	Pinch
	Grated zest of 5 lemons, divided	
2 cups	water	500 mL
1½ cups	freshly squeezed lemon juice	375 mL

TIPS

If you don't have a kitchen scale, you'll need 3 cups (750 mL) pitted sour cherries for this recipe.

For 1½ cups (375 mL) lemon juice, you'll need 8 or 9 lemons.

Prepare the jars and lids.

In a large pot, combine the cherries, sugar, salt, zest of 3 lemons and water. Bring to a boil over medium-high heat, stirring to dissolve the sugar. Reduce the heat and simmer gently, stirring occasionally, for about 15 minutes to coerce the cherries into letting all their juice flow.

Pour the cherry mixture into a fine-mesh sieve set over a deep container. Push down against the cherries to extract as much liquid as possible. Stir the remaining lemon zest and the lemon juice into the syrup.

Pour syrup into the hot jars to within ½ inch (1 cm) of the rim. Wipe rims. Place the lids on the jars and screw the bands on until fingertip-tight. Process in a boiling water canner for 15 minutes.

RED CURRANT SYRUP

I LOVE RED CURRANTS. They are quite seedy, however, so they're often made into jelly rather than jam. I like them best in syrup form — the color is the most beautifully vibrant red. Use it to make Scarlet Pears (page 83) or put a few tablespoons in a champagne flute and top up with sparkling wine for a visually stunning aperitif that's at least as good as kir royale.

Don't omit the citric acid — it's the key to restoring the characteristic acid of the currants, which gets a little lost when cooked.

MAKES ABOUT FOUR JARS (8 OZ/250 ML EACH)

1.8 lbs	stemmed red currants	800 g
2 cups	granulated sugar	400 g
2 cups	water	500 mL
¼ tsp	citric acid	1 mL

TIP

If you don't have a kitchen scale, you'll need 5 cups (1.25 L) stemmed red currants for this recipe.

Prepare the jars and lids.

In a large pot, combine the currants, sugar and water. Bring to a boil over high heat, stirring to dissolve the sugar. Reduce the heat and simmer, stirring often, for 10 minutes.

Pour the currant mixture into a fine-mesh sieve set over a deep container and let drain for 30 minutes. Do not crush the currants or you will end up with a cloudy syrup. Stir the citric acid into the syrup.

Pour syrup into the hot jars to within ½ inch (1 cm) of the rim. Wipe rims. Place the lids on the jars and screw the bands on until fingertip-tight. Process in a boiling water canner for 10 minutes.

STRAWBERRY SYRUP WITH LEMON BALM

THIS SYRUP IS VERY INTENSE. It contains no added water, just the juice of the strawberries. It's great with sparkling water or in a champagne cocktail. I learned this method of making syrup from pastry chef Patrice Demers. It's an excellent way to make the best of strawberries that are a bit past their prime (such as the cheap "jam strawberries" at the market).

MAKES ABOUT THREE JARS (8 OZ/250 ML EACH)

2.7 lbs	strawberries, hulled and halved (or quartered, if large)	1.2 kg
12	sprigs lemon balm (about ½ oz/12 g)	12
1½ cups	granulated sugar	300 g
¾ tsp	citric acid	3 mL
	Additional lemon balm leaves or sprigs (optional)	

TIPS

If you don't have a kitchen scale, you'll need 8 cups (1.9 L) halved hulled strawberries (or quartered, if large) for this recipe.

Feel free to omit the lemon balm or to replace it with another herb. Rose geranium, lavender and anise hyssop are all good options.

If you have a food dehydrator, don't throw away the strawberries after straining out the liquid. You can dry them to make a candy-like snack. Nothing is lost!

In an ample stainless steel bowl, combine the strawberries, lemon balm and sugar. Cover tightly with plastic wrap — it should have a good seal. Place the bowl over a pot half-filled with water (without letting the bottom of the bowl touch the water) and bring the water to a boil over medium heat. Reduce the heat to low and heat for about 1½ hours. The strawberries will slowly release all their juice.

In the meantime, prepare the jars and lids.

Uncover the strawberry mixture and pour it into a fine-mesh sieve set over a deep container. Do not press the strawberries or you will end up with a cloudy syrup. Stir the citric acid into the syrup.

Pour syrup into the hot jars to within ½ inch (1 cm) of the rim. Wipe rims. If desired, place 1 leaf or sprig of lemon balm in each jar, where it will float appealingly. Place the lids on the jars and screw the bands on until fingertip-tight. Process in a boiling water canner for 10 minutes.

SHANDY SYRUP

THIS SYRUP IS INSPIRED BY AN ENGLISH DRINK of beer mixed with lemonade. Instead of beer, I use two ingredients you can find at your local homebrew store: malt syrup and hops. The result is a hoppy, malty, sweet, lemony concoction reminiscent of the cans of nonalcoholic shandy I would drink when I went boating with my father as a child — only better, of course. Try using it to make the Gin Tristram cocktail on page 160.

MAKES THREE OR FOUR JARS (8 OZ/250 ML EACH)

½ cup	granulated sugar	100 g
1 tbsp	grated lemon zest	15 mL
¾ cup + 2 tbsp	water	200 mL
⅓ cup	malt syrup	100 g
¼ cup	dried cascade hops	5 g
¾ cup + 1 tbsp	lemon juice	190 mL

Prepare the jars and lids.

In a medium pot, combine the sugar, lemon zest, water and malt syrup. Bring to a boil over medium-high heat, stirring to dissolve the sugar. Remove from heat and stir in hops. Let soak for 2 minutes (time it, and don't let the hops stay in any longer, or the syrup will become exceedingly bitter).

Pour the hops mixture into a fine-mesh sieve set over a deep container. Stir the lemon juice into the syrup.

Pour syrup into the hot jars to within ½ inch (1 cm) of the rim. Wipe rims. Place the lids on the jars and screw the bands on until fingertip-tight. Process in a boiling water canner for 10 minutes.

CUCUMBER SYRUP WITH MINT AND LIME

THIS IS A REFRESHING, SUMMERY SYRUP. Mix it with seltzer for a spritzer, or try it in a cocktail with rum. It's also great with chilled cantaloupe.

MAKES FOUR OR FIVE JARS (8 OZ/250 ML EACH)

- Blender or food processor
- Jelly bag or cheesecloth-lined sieve

2	English cucumbers (about 1.5 lbs/700 g), cut into chunks	2
⅓ cup	packed fresh mint	20 g
1⅓ cups	granulated sugar	266 g
1⅓ cups	water	325 mL
1 cup	freshly squeezed lime juice	250 mL

In blender, purée cucumbers until smooth.

Transfer the cucumber purée to a damp jelly bag set over a deep container and let drain overnight.

The next day, prepare the jars and lids.

In a small saucepan, combine mint, sugar and water. Bring to a boil over medium-high heat, stirring to dissolve the sugar. Remove from heat and let infuse for 15 minutes. Strain and measure 2 cups (500 mL) syrup. Stir the syrup and lime juice into the cucumber juice.

Pour syrup into the hot jars to within ½ inch (1 cm) of the rim. Wipe rims. Place the lids on the jars and screw the bands on until fingertip-tight. Process in a boiling water canner for 15 minutes.

TIP
For 1 cup (250 mL) lime juice, you'll need 7 to 10 limes.

PICKLES

❧

PICKLES

All kinds of vegetables and fruits can be pickled, and there are a few different ways to do so. Pickles can be fermented or made with vinegar, and the latter may be hot- or fresh-packed. The pickles in this chapter are vinegar pickles. Hot-packing, as explained in the Canned Fruits chapter, means the produce is heated through in the brine before it is packed into jars. This softens and extracts some of the water from the flesh, making it possible to fit more in the jars. For pickles, however, I prefer the fresh-packing method, where the produce is packed raw into the jars and then covered with hot brine. This allows for a more uniform, attractive pack, and also helps to keep the pickles crisp.

Crispness is a very desirable quality in most pickles, and there are a number of ways to achieve it besides a fresh pack. Most importantly, when making cucumber pickles, cut off the blossom end, as it contains an enzyme that will soften the finished product. Brining — in which the prepared produce is layered with ice and coarse salt in a large container, covered with cold water and left overnight — can also enhance crispness, because salt pulls water from the food. But be sure to rinse brined produce well, to avoid overly salty pickles. And always use kosher or pickling salt, as the anti-caking agents in ordinary table salt can lead to cloudiness, which might lead you to mistakenly believe your pickles have gone bad. The minerality of kosher or pickling salt may also increase the crispness of your pickles. Honestly, though, I gave up brining almost entirely when I met calcium chloride, sold by Ball and Bernardin under the brand name Pickle Crisp. It's my secret weapon in the fight against soft pickles. I rarely make a pickle without it, and I find that I can forego brining in its favor.

If I have to, I'll say it a million times: acidity, along with heat processing, is extremely important to the safety of your pickles. Don't alter the amount of vinegar in a recipe, and make sure whatever vinegar you use is a minimum 5% acetic acid. (If you are a true DIYer, this unfortunately means you cannot use your homemade wine vinegar to make pickles.) You can, however, switch up the type of vinegar you use, to get a different flavor. I have a strong preference for cider vinegar, as you'll see, but if you prefer malt vinegar or champagne vinegar, be my guest. You can also play with changing up the spices without compromising the safety of your pickles.

Don't forget, patience is a virtue when it comes to pickles. Let them get to know themselves in your pantry for at least a month before opening a jar. Ideally, wait about 3 months. Pickles will keep for 1 year in a cool, dark place.

BLUE GARLIC

If your pickled garlic turns blue, never fear — that's the result of a normal chemical reaction between the garlic and vinegar. The garlic is still totally safe and delicious to eat.

HORSERADISH SPEARS

HORSERADISH REALLY DESERVES to be star of the show sometimes, as in these slightly sweet pickles, where there are no other spices to get in the way of horseradish's unique hot flavor. Try to find fresh horseradish and grate it yourself — jarred horseradish is often already cured in vinegar and has lost its heat, which manufacturers may compensate for by adding synthetic mustard oil. If you have fresh horseradish left over after making pickles, grate it, pack it into a jar and top with a mixture of equal parts white wine vinegar and water. It will last months in the fridge. Then turn on your oven and make a beef roast, for goodness' sake.

MAKES ABOUT SIX JARS (1 PINT/500 ML EACH)

4.4 lbs	Kirby cucumbers	2 kg

BRINE

1¼ cups	granulated sugar	250 g
2½ tbsp	kosher or pickling salt	37 mL
2 cups	cider vinegar	500 mL
1 cup	water	250 mL

PER JAR

1 tbsp	grated horseradish	15 mL
⅛ tsp	calcium chloride (optional)	0.5 mL

TIPS

If you don't have a kitchen scale, you'll need 48 to 62 Kirby cucumbers for this recipe.

Make sure to wash the cucumbers well, as they can be gritty.

The blossom end of cucumbers contains an enzyme that can make your pickles soft. If you're not sure which is the blossom end, cut both ends off (though here's a hint: it's not the end with the stem).

Prepare the jars and lids.

Trim off the blossom end of the cucumbers. If any cucumbers are longer than 4½ inches (11 cm), trim them to size. Quarter the cucumbers lengthwise to make spears. You should have about 16 cups (3.8 L) spears.

Brine: In a medium saucepan, combine the sugar, salt, vinegar and water. Bring to a boil over high heat, stirring to dissolve the sugar.

Meanwhile, add horseradish and calcium chloride (if using) to the hot jars, then pack in cucumber spears as tightly as possible, leaving a generous ½-inch (1 cm) headspace.

Pour hot brine into the jars to within ½ inch (1 cm) of the rim. Remove any air bubbles, add more brine if necessary and wipe rims. Place the lids on the jars and screw the bands on until fingertip-tight. Process in a boiling water canner for 10 minutes.

DILL PICKLES

TO MY MIND, THESE ARE THE GOLD STANDARD of dill pickles. No, they're not fermented. I love those, too, but I prefer not to compare them. For these, use Kirby cucumbers — little tiny ones or big fat ones, it's your choice. If you choose larger ones, halving or quartering them lengthwise will help you pack the maximum amount into each jar. I've left the amounts open-ended here, so you can make as many or as few jars as you'd like.

MAKES AS MANY 1-QUART (1 L) JARS AS YOUR HEART DESIRES

Kirby cucumbers

BRINE (PER JAR)

1 cup	white vinegar	250 mL
1 cup	water	250 mL

PER JAR

2 to 3	dill heads	2 to 3
2	cloves garlic, peeled	2
1 to 2	hot chile peppers (optional)	1 to 2
1	3-inch (7.5 cm) piece dill root (optional)	1
1 tbsp	kosher or pickling salt	15 mL
2 tsp	mustard seeds	10 mL
1 tsp	whole black peppercorns	5 mL
¼ tsp	calcium chloride	1 mL

Prepare the jars and lids.

Trim off the blossom end of the cucumbers. If the cucumbers are large, halve or quarter them lengthwise.

Brine: In a large pot, combine the vinegar and water. Bring to a boil over high heat. (You will need about 1 cup/250 mL of each for each jar you plan to make.)

Meanwhile, add dill heads, garlic, chiles (if using), dill root (if using), salt, mustard seeds, peppercorns and calcium chloride to the hot jars, then pack in cucumbers as tightly as possible, leaving a generous ½-inch (1 cm) headspace.

Pour hot brine into the jars to within ½ inch (1 cm) of the rim. Remove any air bubbles, add more liquid if necessary and wipe rims. Place the lids on the jars and screw the bands on until fingertip-tight. Process in a boiling water canner for 15 minutes.

TIPS

Make sure to wash the cucumbers well, as they can be gritty.

The blossom end of cucumbers contains an enzyme that can make your pickles soft. Ugh! If you're not sure which is the blossom end, cut both ends off (though here's a hint: it's not the end with the stem).

It's best to make batch sizes that will fit in your canner in one load. Extra jars will cool too much while the first full load is processing in the canner.

MALT PICKLED CAULIFLOWER

MALT VINEGAR HAS ALWAYS BEEN one of my favorites — I do have a British father, after all. Mellow cauliflower takes well to it, and the addition of buckwheat honey rounds it out with an earthy sweetness. These are really good on a charcuterie plate or thrown into a salad.

MAKES ABOUT SEVEN JARS (1 PINT/500 ML EACH)

BRINE

1 cup	packed brown sugar	220 g
7 tbsp	kosher or pickling salt	105 mL
5 cups	malt vinegar	1.25 L
2 cups	water	500 mL
1 cup	buckwheat honey	350 g

PER JAR

3	allspice berries	3
2	whole cloves	2
1	clove garlic, peeled	1
½ tsp	whole black peppercorns	2 mL
½ tsp	hot pepper flakes	2 mL
½ tsp	mustard seeds	2 mL
¼ tsp	calcium chloride	1 mL
2.8 lbs	cauliflower florets	1.25 kg
12 oz	pearl onions, peeled (see tips, at right)	350 g

Prepare the jars and lids.

Brine: In a large saucepan, combine the brown sugar, salt, vinegar, water and honey. Bring to a boil over high heat, stirring to dissolve the sugar.

Meanwhile, add allspice, cloves, garlic, peppercorns, hot pepper flakes, mustard seeds and a heaping ¼ tsp (1 mL) calcium chloride to the hot jars, then pack in cauliflower and pearl onions as tightly as possible, leaving a generous ½-inch (1 cm) headspace.

Pour hot brine into the jars to within ½ inch (1 cm) of the rim. Remove any air bubbles, add more brine if necessary and wipe rims. Place the lids on the jars and screw the bands on until fingertip-tight. Process in a boiling water canner for 10 minutes.

TIPS

If you don't have a kitchen scale, you'll need 11 cups (2.6 L) cauliflower florets and 3 cups (750 mL) pearl onions for this recipe.

To easily peel pearl onions, snip both ends off, cover with boiling water and wait 20 seconds. Drain and rinse under cold water, then slip the onions out of their skins.

MAPLE GINGER PICKLED BEETS

MAPLE SYRUP AND ROOT VEGETABLES are two of the few local products that are easy to find during the long winter months in Quebec. Fortunately, they complement each other. I usually find pickled beets too sweet. Maple syrup adds a more subtle sweetness, with its own flavor, to the earthy beets. A little ginger brings a high note of spiciness.

MAKES ABOUT SIX JARS (1 PINT/500 ML EACH)

4 lbs	beets (about 22 small to medium)	1.8 kg

BRINE

3½ cups	cider vinegar	875 mL
1½ cups	pure maple syrup	375 mL
1½ cups	water	375 mL
2 tsp	pickling salt	10 mL

PER JAR

2	gingerroot coins	2
¼ tsp	ground ginger	1 mL
¼ tsp	dry mustard	1 mL
¼ tsp	whole black peppercorns	1 mL
⅛ tsp	allspice berries	0.5 mL

Trim the beets and scrub them well. Place them in a large pot and cover with water. Cover and bring to a boil over high heat. Reduce heat and simmer until just tender. This will take anywhere from 20 to 45 minutes, depending on the size of your beets.

In the meantime, prepare the jars and lids.

Drain the beets, then run cold water over them until they're cool enough to handle. You should now be able to slip the skins right off. Once they're all peeled, halve or quarter the beets if large.

Brine: In a large saucepan, combine the vinegar, maple syrup, water and salt. Bring to a boil over high heat.

Meanwhile, add gingerroot coins, ground ginger, mustard, peppercorns and allspice to the hot jars, then pack in beets as tightly as possible, leaving a generous ½-inch (1 cm) headspace.

Pour hot brine into the jars to within ½ inch (1 cm) of the rim. Remove any air bubbles, add more brine if necessary and wipe rims. Place the lids on the jars and screw the bands on until fingertip-tight. Process in a boiling water canner for 30 minutes.

HEARTBEETS

MY DEAR FRIEND KINNERET HAD THE GENIUS IDEA for these heart-shaped beet pickles, and I helped her prepare them for our friend Nora's birthday. We went with a simple spicing and used pink beets, whose color is light enough that you can clearly see the heart shapes in the jar (standard red beets will produce a liquid that is too dark).

I really wanted to offer these as a regular Preservation Society product, but when I realized the insane amount of time it took to make them in large volumes, I had to resign myself to reserving them solely for Valentine's Day.

MAKES ABOUT TWO JARS (1 PINT/500 ML EACH)

- Heart-shaped cookie cutters in various sizes

4.4 lbs	beets, preferably pink (about 24 small to medium)	2 kg

BRINE

2 cups	white wine vinegar	500 mL
½ cup	water	125 mL
1 tbsp	granulated sugar	15 mL
2 tsp	kosher or pickling salt	10 mL

PER JAR

½ tsp	whole pink peppercorns	2 mL
½ tsp	whole black peppercorns	2 mL
½ tsp	juniper berries	2 mL

TIPS

You'll end up with a lot of beet scraps — don't throw them away! Make a soup.

If you're not feeling romantic, you can cut the beets into alphabet or number shapes, which children will find extremely charming.

Trim the beets and scrub them well. Place them in a pot and cover with water. Cover and bring to a boil over high heat. Reduce heat and simmer until just tender. This will take anywhere from 20 to 45 minutes, depending on the size of your beets.

In the meantime, prepare the jars and lids.

Drain the beets, then run cold water over them until they're cool enough to handle. You should now be able to slip the skins right off. Cut the peeled beets into ¾-inch (2 cm) thick slices, then use the cookie cutters to cut out heart shapes (see tip, at left).

Brine: In a small saucepan, combine the vinegar, water, sugar and salt. Bring to a boil over high heat.

Meanwhile, add pink peppercorns, black peppercorns and juniper berries to the hot jars, then pack in beets as tightly as possible, leaving a generous ½-inch (1 cm) headspace.

Pour hot brine into the jars to within ½ inch (1 cm) of the rim. Remove any air bubbles, add more brine if necessary and wipe rims. Place the lids on the jars and screw the bands on until fingertip-tight. Process in a boiling water canner for 30 minutes.

PICKLED BRUSSELS SPROUTS

THESE ARE SO CUTE! Why aren't pickled Brussels sprouts more common? They look like tiny whole sauerkraut. The best thing I've ever done with these was simple (as so many good things are). Roast a tray of potato chunks, scatter quartered pickled Brussels sprouts around them, then cover in cheese (I typically use Cheddar or Parmesan) and return to the oven for a few minutes to melt. *Voilà!* — a perfect side dish.

MAKES ABOUT SIX JARS (1 PINT/500 ML EACH)

3 lbs	Brussels sprouts	1.4 kg

BRINE

2½ cups	cider vinegar	625 mL
2½ cups	water	625 mL
2 tbsp	kosher or pickling salt	30 mL

PER JAR

1	clove garlic, peeled	1
1 tsp	mustard seeds	5 mL
½ tsp	hot pepper flakes	2 mL
½ tsp	whole black peppercorns	2 mL
⅛ tsp	calcium chloride	0.5 mL

Prepare the jars and lids.

Trim the Brussels sprouts and remove any discolored, loose or tough outer leaves. Halve them if large. You should have 2.8 lbs (1.25 kg) or 10 cups (2.4 L).

Brine: In a large saucepan, combine the vinegar, water and salt. Bring to a boil over high heat.

Meanwhile, add garlic, mustard seeds, hot pepper flakes, peppercorns and calcium chloride to the hot jars, then pack in Brussels sprouts as tightly as possible, leaving a generous ½-inch (1 cm) headspace.

Pour hot brine into the jars to within ½ inch (1 cm) of the rim. Remove any air bubbles, add more brine if necessary and wipe rims. Place the lids on the jars and screw the bands on until fingertip-tight. Process in a boiling water canner for 10 minutes.

DILLY GREEN BEANS

SOMETIMES YOU NEED A CHANGE from a dill pickle; sometimes you just want a dill bean. These make a great cocktail garnish, thrown into a bloody Caesar or a martini.

MAKES ABOUT FIVE JARS (1 PINT/500 ML EACH)

BRINE

2 cups	rice vinegar	500 mL
2 cups	white vinegar	500 mL
2 cups	water	500 mL
3 tbsp	kosher or pickling salt	45 mL

PER JAR

2	dill heads	2
1 to 2	cloves garlic, peeled	1 to 2
$\frac{1}{4}$ tsp	whole black peppercorns	1 mL
$\frac{1}{8}$ tsp	calcium chloride	0.5 mL
2.2 lbs	green beans (see tips, at right)	1 kg

Prepare the jars and lids.

Brine: In a large saucepan, combine the rice vinegar, white vinegar, water and salt. Bring to a boil over high heat.

Meanwhile, add dill heads, garlic, peppercorns and calcium chloride to the hot jars, then pack in beans as tightly as possible, leaving a generous $\frac{1}{2}$-inch (1 cm) headspace.

Pour hot brine into the jars to within $\frac{1}{2}$ inch (1 cm) of the rim. Remove any air bubbles, add more brine if necessary and wipe rims. Place the lids on the jars and screw the bands on until fingertip-tight. Process in a boiling water canner for 10 minutes.

TIPS

If you don't have a kitchen scale, you'll need 8 cups (1.9 L) green beans for this recipe.

If you like, you can remove the stems from the beans, but I don't bother. I like a stem — it's nature's handle.

SPICY PICKLED OKRA

MANY YEARS AGO, I BOUGHT A JAR of Rick's Picks pickled okra at a farmers' market. It was pickled with smoked paprika, which was such a great idea that I stole it. The person manning the booth suggested wrapping the pickles in thinly sliced serrano ham, and they were right — they're delicious that way and make an original accompaniment to an aperitif. These pickles are good in almost everything, though, especially Mexican food.

Okra isn't super-popular in many areas, even though you can get it fresh at the farmers' market at the same time that the abundance of peppers and tomatoes appears. Some people may leave okra pickles uneaten on an assortment platter simply because they don't know what they are. Others are averse to okra because it can have a slimy texture — but pickling totally eliminates that. I urge you to give okra pickles a try if you aren't already in love with them.

MAKES ABOUT FIVE JARS (1 PINT/500 ML EACH)

BRINE

4 cups	cider vinegar	1 L
2 cups	water	500 mL
3 tbsp	kosher or pickling salt	45 mL

PER JAR

1	clove garlic, peeled	1
1	small red chile pepper	1
1 tsp	hot smoked paprika	5 mL
½ tsp	whole black peppercorns	2 mL
½ tsp	cayenne pepper	2 mL
⅛ tsp	calcium chloride	0.5 mL
1 to 2 tbsp	hot pepper sauce (such as Frank's Red Hot)	15 to 30 mL
2.2 lbs	okra, trimmed	1 kg

Prepare the jars and lids.

Brine: In a large saucepan, combine the vinegar, water and salt. Bring to a boil over high heat.

Meanwhile, add garlic, chiles, paprika, peppercorns, cayenne, calcium chloride and hot pepper sauce to taste to the hot jars, then pack in okra as tightly as possible, leaving a generous ½-inch (1 cm) headspace.

Pour hot brine into the jars to within ½ inch (1 cm) of the rim. Remove any air bubbles, add more brine if necessary and wipe rims. Place the lids on the jars and screw the bands on until fingertip-tight. Process in a boiling water canner for 10 minutes.

> **TIP**
>
> If you don't have a kitchen scale, you'll need 10 cups (2.4 L) okra for this recipe.

MAPLE CHILE ONIONS

THIS IS AN IDEA I BIT FROM EBEN FREEMAN, mixologist extraordinaire. One night, when I was eating at wd~50 in NYC, where he tended bar at the time, he served me the most crazily delicious gin, Old Raj, garnished with his own maple chile pickled onions. It blew my mind, and when I got back to Montreal I immediately recreated the onions. (I couldn't afford the gin!) These really amp up a Dirty Gibson (see page 160) or a plain glass of gin, but would be equally welcome with a cheese or charcuterie plate. Dare I say ploughman's lunch?

I like pickled onions, and my parents adore them, but I had to stop producing them for sale because they are so time-consuming to make in large volumes. That said, it's totally worth making a small batch for gifts and personal consumption — they are infinitely more delicious than the ones on supermarket shelves.

MAKES ABOUT FOUR JARS (8 OZ/250 ML EACH)

BRINE

1½ cups	cider vinegar	375 mL
½ cup	pure maple syrup	125 mL
1½ tbsp	kosher or pickling salt	22 mL

PER JAR

1	bay leaf	1
1	small red chile pepper	1
½ tsp	whole black peppercorns (preferably smoked)	2 mL
½ tsp	mustard seeds	2 mL
½ tsp	hot pepper flakes (preferable chipotle pepper flakes)	2 mL
¼ tsp	smoked paprika (hot or sweet)	1 mL
Pinch	calcium chloride	Pinch
1.7 lbs	pearl onions, peeled (see tips, at right)	750 g

Prepare the jars and lids.

Brine: In a small saucepan, combine the vinegar, maple syrup and salt. Bring to a boil over high heat.

Meanwhile, add bay leaves, chiles, peppercorns, mustard seeds, hot pepper flakes, paprika and calcium chloride to the hot jars, then gently pack in onions as tightly as possible, leaving a generous ½-inch (1 cm) headspace.

Pour hot brine into the jars to within ½ inch (1 cm) of the rim. Remove any air bubbles, add more brine if necessary and wipe rims. Place the lids on the jars and screw the bands on until fingertip-tight. Process in a boiling water canner for 10 minutes.

TIPS

If you don't have a kitchen scale, you'll need 6½ cups (1.6 L) pearl onions for this recipe.

To easily peel pearl onions, snip both ends off, cover with boiling water and wait 20 seconds. Drain and rinse under cold water, then slip the onions out of their skins.

PICKLED RAISINS

A NUMBER OF YEARS AGO, I bought a jar of pickled raisins at a cool shop in New York, and I've been meaning to make my own version ever since. Here it is! These sour little flavor bombs are ideal for cutting richness and would make a fantastic accompaniment to a terrine.

MAKES ABOUT SIX JARS (8 OZ/250 ML EACH)

2¼ cups	cider vinegar	550 mL
1½ cups	water	375 mL
2 tsp	kosher or pickling salt	10 mL
1.8 lbs	golden raisins	800 g

PER JAR

1	2-inch (5 cm) sprig fresh rosemary	1
1	bay leaf	1
1 tsp	mustard seeds	5 mL
½ tsp	hot pepper flakes	2 mL
¼ tsp	allspice berries	1 mL

In a large pot, combine the vinegar, water and salt. Bring to a boil over high heat. Remove from heat and add raisins. Cover and let stand until the raisins are quite plump, about 1 hour.

In the meantime, prepare the jars and lids.

Add rosemary, bay leaves, mustard seeds, hot pepper flakes and allspice to the hot jars, then, using a slotted spoon, fill the jars with raisins, leaving a generous ½-inch (1 cm) headspace.

Bring the brine back to a boil. Pour hot brine into the jars to within ½ inch (1 cm) of the rim. Remove any air bubbles, add more brine if necessary and wipe rims. Place the lids on the jars and screw the bands on until fingertip-tight. Process in a boiling water canner for 10 minutes.

> **TIP**
>
> If you don't have a kitchen scale, you'll need 5¼ cups (1.3 L) golden raisins for this recipe.

PICKLED POBLANO PEPPERS

POBLANO PEPPERS ARE ONE OF MY FAVORITE VARIETIES. You can find them year-round, but I like to make these pickles in September, with freshly harvested poblanos. I halve the peppers for versatility, but you can also slice them into strips. These pickles vastly improve tacos, nachos and quesadillas.

MAKES ABOUT THREE JARS (1 PINT/500 ML EACH)

- Preheat barbecue grill to high, or preheat broiler

3.3 lbs	poblano peppers (16 to 18 medium)	1.5 kg
1¾ cups	cider vinegar	425 mL
½ cup	water	125 mL
1 tbsp	honey	15 mL
1 tsp	kosher or pickling salt	5 mL
3	cloves garlic, smashed	3
3	bay leaves	3

TIP

While poblanos are generally quite mild, it's still a good idea to wear rubber gloves when you're handling them, as the occasional hot one can burn your hands.

Grill or broil the poblanos until the skins are blackened but the peppers still hold their shape. Enclose them in a paper bag or plastic container for 10 minutes. When they are cool enough to handle, peel off the skins, halve the peppers and remove the seeds.

In the meantime, prepare the jars and lids.

In a small saucepan, combine the vinegar, water, honey and salt. Bring to a boil over high heat.

Meanwhile, pack poblanos into the hot jars, leaving a generous ½-inch (1 cm) headspace. Top each with 1 garlic clove and 1 bay leaf.

Pour hot brine into the jars to within ½ inch (1 cm) of the rim. Remove any air bubbles, add more brine if necessary and wipe rims. Place the lids on the jars and screw the bands on until fingertip-tight. Process in a boiling water canner for 15 minutes.

SPRING MIX

I HAVE DECIDED TO REAPPROPRIATE the term "spring mix" for this pretty, simple pickle of radishes and white asparagus in a tarragon-scented brine. I love spring, so I don't like that "spring mix" is used to describe the ubiquitous prepackaged mesclun that is often slimy and is available year-round. This pickle, on the other hand, is for making when the first spring vegetables of the year arrive at the market. You don't have to use white asparagus, but red radishes bleed their color and turn the brine pink, and when you use green asparagus, it can look a little too Christmassy.

Try adding these pickles to a salad of hard-cooked eggs and baby lettuce.

MAKES ABOUT THREE JARS (1 PINT/500 ML EACH)

13 oz	white asparagus (about 2 bunches), cut into 1-inch (2.5 cm) pieces	365 g
11 oz	radishes (about ½ bunch), halved or quartered if large	320 g

BRINE

2 cups	white balsamic vinegar	500 mL
1 cup	water	250 mL
1½ tsp	pickling salt	7 mL

PER JAR

1	sprig fresh tarragon	1
1 tbsp	minced shallot	15 mL
¼ tsp	celery seeds	1 mL
¼ tsp	dill seeds	1 mL
⅛ tsp	calcium chloride	0.5 mL
1 tbsp	dry vermouth	15 mL

Prepare the jars and lids.

In a large bowl, toss the asparagus and radishes until evenly combined.

Brine: In a small saucepan, combine the vinegar, water and salt. Bring to a boil over high heat.

Meanwhile, add tarragon, shallot, celery seeds, dill seeds, calcium chloride and vermouth to the hot jars, then pack in vegetables as tightly as possible, leaving a generous ½-inch (1 cm) headspace.

Pour hot brine into the jars to within ½ inch (1 cm) of the rim. Remove any air bubbles, add more brine if necessary and wipe rims. Place the lids on the jars and screw the bands on until fingertip-tight. Process in a boiling water canner for 10 minutes.

> **TIP**
>
> If you don't have a kitchen scale, you'll need 3 cups (750 mL) chopped asparagus and about 8 red radishes for this recipe.

MISO MIXED PICKLE

I LOVE A MIXED PICKLE — it's like a party in a jar. So good-looking! So diverse! This one is crunchy and bright and can hold its own as a snack, though it's also very attractive on a sandwich.

MAKES ABOUT FIVE JARS (1 PINT/500 ML EACH)

7 oz	corn on the cob (1 cob), quartered lengthwise and cut into 1-inch (2.5 cm) chunks	200 g
5 oz	cauliflower florets	150 g
5 oz	daikon radishes, cut into ½-inch (1 cm) chunks	150 g
4 oz	mini bell peppers, slit or halved if large	120 g
3½ oz	green beans, cut into 1-inch (2.5 cm) pieces	100 g
2½ oz	shimeji mushrooms	70 g
2 oz	finger chile peppers (about 4), cut into 1-inch (2.5 cm) chunks	50 g

BRINE

½ cup	granulated sugar	100 g
1 tbsp	pickling salt	15 mL
3 cups	white wine vinegar	750 mL
2 cups	water	500 mL
⅓ cup	shiro miso	120 g

PER JAR

2	gingerroot coins	2
1	clove garlic, peeled	1
1 tsp	mustard seeds	5 mL
¼ tsp	whole black peppercorns	1 mL
⅛ tsp	calcium chloride	0.5 mL

Prepare the jars and lids.

In a large bowl, toss the corn, cauliflower, radishes, bell peppers, green beans, mushrooms and chiles. You want to combine them well, to ensure that you have a little of everything in each jar.

Brine: In a medium saucepan, combine the sugar, salt, vinegar and water. Bring to a boil over high heat, stirring to dissolve the sugar. Remove from heat and whisk in the miso, making sure it dissolves.

Meanwhile, add ginger, garlic, mustard seeds, peppercorns and calcium chloride to the hot jars, then pack in vegetables as tightly as possible, leaving a generous ½-inch (1 cm) headspace.

Pour hot brine into the jars to within ½ inch (1 cm) of the rim. Remove any air bubbles, add more brine if necessary and wipe rims. Place the lids on the jars and screw the bands on until fingertip-tight. Process in a boiling water canner for 10 minutes.

TIPS

If you don't have a kitchen scale, you'll need 2 cups (500 mL) cauliflower florets, 1 cup (250 mL) chopped daikon radish, 1½ cups (375 mL) mini bell peppers, 1 cup (250 mL) sliced green beans and 1 cup (250 mL) shimeji mushrooms.

If you can't find shimeji mushrooms, try small button mushrooms or torn oyster mushrooms.

CHUTNEYS, RELISHES AND SAVORY JAMS

CHUTNEYS, RELISHES AND SAVORY JAMS

During the second canning class I ever taught, the well-intentioned organizer asked me, in front of a roomful of strangers, what the difference was between a chutney and a relish. I was speechless. I've thought about it a good amount since then, though I'm not sure why — the words are often used interchangeably. Still, this is what I've come up with:

◊ A chutney is basically a pickle-jam hybrid. A pickled jam, if you will. It's a sour-sweet condiment with roots in India that really caught on with the Brits. It is delicious with cheeses and meats, as is or between slices of bread. Generally, a chutney is made with finely chopped fruit mixed with onions, spices, salt, sugar and vinegar. This mixture is cooked down slowly until it reaches a jam-like consistency.

◊ A relish is what North Americans are more accustomed to. I like to think of it as a bunch of tiny pickles in a brine that's just a bit thicker than usual. More often made with vegetables, as in the classic cucumber relish, it's a tangy, chunky condiment used to embellish burgers, hot dogs and other foods.

You'll also find some savory jams in this chapter. These aren't exactly chutney or relish — or even jam, really. They're salty, they're spreadable and they're good. That's really all you need to know.

As with pickles, it's important not to adjust the amount of vinegar in these recipes — it's crucial for the proper acidification of the preserve.

It's best to wait at least a month after canning chutneys, relishes and savory jams before eating them. This gives the intense flavors time to mature and come into their own. Chutneys, relishes and savory jams will keep for 1 year in a cool, dark place.

A WORD OF WARNING

When you make chutney and, to a lesser extent, relish, the aroma will pervade your entire house (and hair and clothes) and may make people mad at you. (I know this from experience.) They will probably forgive you when they try it, though.

FAMOUS APPLE CHUTNEY

I CALL THIS CHUTNEY FAMOUS because, for a while, everyone I knew in a five-block radius was a bit obsessed with it, and for good reason. Its tangy sweetness and spicy finish elevate a standard grilled cheese sandwich or burger to something pretty VIP. It even makes a piece of leftover chicken eaten cold in front of the fridge feel like a bit of an event.

MAKES ABOUT SIX JARS (8 OZ/250 ML EACH)

4 to 5	red Thai chile peppers (or other small red chiles), finely chopped	4 to 5
3	cloves garlic, finely chopped	3
2 lbs	apples (about 6 medium), finely chopped	900 g
1 lb	onions (about 2 large), finely chopped	450 g
6 oz	raisins	170 g
2½ cups	packed dark brown sugar	550 g
2 tbsp	grated gingerroot	30 mL
1½ tbsp	kosher or pickling salt	22 mL
2 tsp	ground allspice	10 mL
2 tsp	ground cloves	10 mL
2 tsp	freshly ground black pepper	10 mL
2 tsp	ground turmeric	10 mL
½ tsp	dry mustard	2 mL
1½ cups	cider vinegar	375 mL
1½ cups	malt vinegar	375 mL

Prepare the jars and lids.

In a large, heavy-bottomed pot, combine the chiles, garlic, apples, onions, raisins, brown sugar, ginger, salt, allspice, cloves, pepper, turmeric, mustard, cider vinegar and malt vinegar. Bring to a boil over medium-high heat, stirring to dissolve the sugar. Reduce the heat and simmer, stirring occasionally and gradually reducing the heat, until the mixture thickens to a jammy consistency. This should take about 1 hour. Remove from heat.

Ladle chutney into the hot jars to within ½ inch (1 cm) of the rim. Remove any air bubbles and wipe rims. Place the lids on the jars and screw the bands on until fingertip-tight. Process in a boiling water canner for 10 minutes.

TIPS

You can finely chop the apples, onions, chiles and garlic by hand, but you may as well use a food processor, if you have one. Everything is going to meld together anyway, so precisely dicing your produce isn't really worth it.

If you don't have a kitchen scale, you'll need 1 cup (250 mL) raisins for this recipe.

If you cannot find malt vinegar, cider vinegar can be used in its place.

DEVIL'S CHUTNEY

THIS CHUTNEY WAS DEVELOPED BY ANTHONY KINIK, my friend, an extraordinary cook and writer, and half of the duo behind the definitive Montreal food blog "... an endless banquet." I feel very lucky that he was generous enough to let me include this recipe — it is my all-time favorite chutney! I feel like the king of the world now that I can make it whenever I want. It is so good on everything, but I particularly like it in a grilled cheese sandwich. Watch out if you're averse to spice, though — you might want to use fewer chiles, or at least a milder variety.

MAKES ABOUT SIX JARS (8 OZ/250 ML EACH)

- Food processor

3 tbsp	olive oil	45 mL
1.3 lbs	onions (about 3 medium), finely chopped	600 g
6	chile peppers (red or green, or Scotch bonnet, if you dare)	6
3	cloves garlic	3
1	4-inch (10 cm) piece gingerroot	1
2.2 lbs	raisins	1 kg
6 tbsp	granulated sugar	75 g
1 tbsp	kosher or pickling salt	15 mL
1½ tsp	chili powder	7 mL
½ tsp	cayenne powder	2 mL
2½ cups	malt vinegar	625 mL
¾ cup	tamarind purée (see box, opposite)	175 mL
½ cup	dark rum	125 mL

Prepare the jars and lids.

In a large pot, heat the oil over medium heat. Add the onions and cook, stirring, until they begin to color. Remove from heat.

In a food processor, finely chop the chiles, garlic and ginger. Add the raisins, sugar, salt, chili powder, cayenne, vinegar, tamarind purée and rum; purée until smooth. (You may have to do this in batches, unless you have a huge food processor.)

Add the purée to the onions and bring to a boil over high heat. Cook, stirring often and gradually reducing the heat, until the mixture thickens to a jammy consistency. This should take 20 to 30 minutes. Remove from heat.

Ladle chutney into the hot jars to within ½ inch (1 cm) of the rim. Remove any air bubbles and wipe rims. Place the lids on the jars and screw the bands on until fingertip-tight. Process in a boiling water canner for 10 minutes.

TAMARIND PURÉE

Anthony explains: To make tamarind purée out of a block of tamarind pulp (around here, these usually come in bricks weighing 8 oz/250 g, which is exactly what you need for this formula), you need to break the block into little pieces as best you can, then pour 2 cups (500 mL) of hot water over top, cover and let stand overnight. The next day, you just pass the softened tamarind pulp and liquid through a sieve, smashing the pulp against the mesh with a wooden spoon to extract as much tamarind goodness as possible. Make sure to scrape the tamarind purée from the underside of the sieve. Place the tamarind purée in a jar and refrigerate it. You now have the base ingredient for a whole host of Thai, Indian, West Indian and Central American dishes.

CRANBERRY SAUCE

I SUPPOSE THIS IS TECHNICALLY A JAM, but since I use it almost exclusively as I would a chutney, it ended up in this chapter. I have always adored cranberry sauce — as a child, I would often have more of it on my plate at Thanksgiving than any other food, even though it was just the commercial variety. This cranberry sauce makes me want to act like a kid again. It's so good I always make sure to have more than one jar on hand if we're going to be eating turkey.

MAKES FOUR OR FIVE JARS (8 OZ/250 ML EACH)

2.2 lbs	cranberries	1 kg
3¼ cups	granulated sugar	650 g
1	3-inch (7.5 cm) cinnamon stick	1
1	whole star anise	1
¼ tsp	ground cloves	1 mL
	Grated zest and juice of 2 large oranges	
6 tbsp	port (optional)	90 mL

> **TIP**
>
> If you don't have a kitchen scale, you'll need 9 cups (2.1 L) cranberries for this recipe.

Prepare the jars and lids.

In a large pot or preserving pan, combine the cranberries, sugar, cinnamon, star anise, cloves, orange zest and orange juice. Cook over medium heat, stirring occasionally, until, after 10 minutes or so, the cranberries begin to pop. (What a satisfying sound!) Increase the heat to medium-high and boil hard, stirring often, until the setting point is reached (see page 17). Remove from heat and let rest for 5 minutes, stirring occasionally. Discard the cinnamon stick and star anise. Stir in the port, if using.

Ladle sauce into the hot jars to within ¼ inch (0.5 cm) of the rim. Remove any air bubbles and wipe rims. Place the lids on the jars and screw the bands on until fingertip-tight. Process in a boiling water canner for 10 minutes.

DRIED FRUIT MOSTARDA

MOSTARDA IS AN ITALIAN CONDIMENT of fruit in mustard syrup, often served with meats and cheeses. I hadn't thought to make it until a client approached me to develop an exclusive version. This recipe is in much the same vein. I would by no means claim this is a traditional mostarda, but it's definitely delicious. It's also made entirely of pantry items, which are always in season, so you can make it anytime.

MAKES ABOUT THREE JARS (8 OZ/250 ML EACH)

1 cup	granulated sugar	200 g
3 cups	water	750 mL
2	bay leaves	2
5½ oz	chopped dried apricots	160 g
5 oz	chopped dried pears	150 g
5 oz	golden raisins	150 g
4 oz	dried cranberries	110 g
3 tbsp	dry mustard	45 mL
2 tbsp	mustard seeds	30 mL
1½ tsp	kosher or pickling salt	7 mL
⅓ cup	white wine vinegar	75 mL

Prepare the jars and lids.

In a medium, heavy-bottomed saucepan, combine the sugar and water. Bring to a boil over high heat, stirring to dissolve the sugar. Add the bay leaves, apricots, pears, raisins and cranberries; reduce the heat and simmer, stirring occasionally, until the fruit is plump and rehydrated, about 10 minutes. Add the dry mustard, mustard seeds, salt and vinegar; increase the heat slightly and simmer, stirring occasionally, until the mixture is thick and syrupy, about 10 minutes. Remove from heat and discard the bay leaves.

Ladle mostarda into the hot jars to within ½ inch (1 cm) of the rim. Remove any air bubbles and wipe rims. Place the lids on the jars and screw the bands on until fingertip-tight. Process in a boiling water canner for 10 minutes.

TIPS

If you don't have a kitchen scale, you'll need 1 cup (250 mL) each of the apricots, pears, raisins and cranberries for this recipe.

Feel free to use different combinations of dried fruits. Just keep the total amount to about 1.2 lbs (550 g) or 4 cups (1 L).

CUCUMBER RELISH WITH FENNEL AND MEYER LEMON

SWEET, SOUR AND VEGETAL — these are the tastes that make relish great. Unfortunately, the dominant flavor in many store-bought relishes is chemicals. Fortunately, it's a cinch to make your own, as long as you can dice a vegetable. This one is a highbrow-lowbrow champ, as good on poached fish as it is on a hot dog.

MAKES ABOUT FIVE JARS (8 OZ/250 ML EACH)

2	Meyer lemons	2
½ cup	granulated sugar	100 g
1½ tsp	kosher or pickling salt	7 mL
1½ cups	champagne vinegar	375 mL
1.3 lbs	Kirby cucumbers, finely diced	600 g
11 oz	fennel bulb (1 medium), finely diced	300 g
4½ oz	onion, finely chopped	130 g
1 tsp	celery seeds	5 mL
1 tsp	wild fennel seeds	5 mL
1 tsp	freshly cracked black pepper	5 mL
1 tsp	cracked juniper berries	5 mL
2	pinches calcium chloride	2

Prepare the jars and lids.

Remove the zest from the lemons with a vegetable peeler, then slice the zest into fine julienne. Juice the lemons as well.

In a large pot, combine the sugar, salt and vinegar. Bring to a boil over high heat, stirring to dissolve the sugar. Add the lemon zest, lemon juice, cucumbers, fennel, onion, celery seeds, fennel seeds, pepper, juniper berries and calcium chloride; bring back to a rolling boil. Immediately remove from heat.

Ladle relish into the hot jars to within ½ inch (1 cm) of the rim. Remove any air bubbles and wipe rims. Place the lids on the jars and screw the bands on until fingertip-tight. Process in a boiling water canner for 10 minutes.

> ### TIP
>
> If you don't have a kitchen scale, you'll need 4 cups (1 L) finely diced cucumbers, 2 cups (500 mL) finely diced fennel bulb and 1 cup (250 mL) finely chopped onion for this recipe.

GRANDMA'S RHUBARB RELISH

A FEW YEARS AGO I GOT A DESPERATE EMAIL from my Aunt Della. She was searching for the recipe for my grandmother Molly's rhubarb chutney, which she remembered fondly and felt she must eat. I was intrigued — I don't remember ever having tried it, but if my grandma made it, there's no way it wasn't good. Fortunately, Della finally dug up the recipe, and now I can share it with you.

MAKES ABOUT SEVEN JARS (8 OZ/250 ML EACH)

3.3 lbs	rhubarb, cut into ½-inch (1 cm) pieces	1.5 kg
1.3 lbs	onions (2 large), finely chopped	600 g
2 cups	malt vinegar	500 mL
3 cups	packed brown sugar	660 g
2 tsp	ground ginger	10 mL
2 tsp	ground cinnamon	10 mL
1½ tsp	kosher or pickling salt	7 mL
½ tsp	ground cloves	2 mL
½ tsp	ground allspice	2 mL

Prepare the jars and lids.

In a large nonreactive pot, combine the rhubarb, onions and vinegar. Cook over medium-high heat for 20 minutes or until the rhubarb and onions are soft. Add the brown sugar, ginger, cinnamon, salt, cloves and allspice; cook, stirring occasionally and gradually reducing the heat, until the mixture thickens to a jammy consistency, about 45 minutes. Remove from heat.

Ladle relish into the hot jars to within ½ inch (1 cm) of the rim. Remove any air bubbles and wipe rims. Place the lids on the jars and screw the bands on until fingertip-tight. Process in a boiling water canner for 10 minutes.

TIPS

If you don't have a kitchen scale, you'll need 12 cups (2.8 L) chopped rhubarb and 4⅔ cups (1.2 L) chopped onions for this recipe.

If you cannot find malt vinegar, cider vinegar can be used in its place.

ONION BEER JAM

WHAT MORE COULD YOU REALLY WANT to enliven your burger, grilled cheese sandwich or sausage? Or, indeed, your poutine (see page 168). Just be sure to use a mellow beer — preferably a brown or red ale. I generally prefer to drink something hoppier, but the bitterness of hops is jarring and out of place in this context.

MAKES ABOUT THREE JARS (8 OZ/250 ML EACH)

3 tbsp	unsalted butter	45 mL
2.2 lbs	onions (4 to 5 medium), thinly sliced	1 kg
½ cup	packed brown sugar	110 g
1½ tsp	kosher or pickling salt	7 mL
½ tsp	freshly ground black pepper	2 mL
1	bottle (12 oz/341 mL) beer (brown or red ale)	1
¾ cup	malt vinegar	175 mL
2 tbsp	malt syrup	30 mL

Prepare the jars and lids.

In a medium pot, melt the butter over medium heat. Add the onions and cook, stirring occasionally and reducing the heat as necessary, until golden and melty. Add the brown sugar, salt, pepper, beer, vinegar and malt syrup; increase the heat to medium-high and cook, stirring often, until the mixture thickens to a jammy consistency. This should take 20 to 30 minutes.

Ladle jam into the hot jars to within ½ inch (1 cm) of the rim. Remove any air bubbles and wipe rims. Place the lids on the jars and screw the bands on until fingertip-tight. Process in a boiling water canner for 15 minutes.

TIPS

If you don't have a kitchen scale, you'll need 9 cups (2.1 L) thinly sliced onions for this recipe.

If you cannot find malt vinegar, cider vinegar can be used in its place.

It is unusual to include butter in home canning recipes, but this recipe has been safety-tested to ensure the correct pH and processing time. Do not attempt to use fats or animal products in other recipes that have not been tested. For food safety, this recipe must be prepared exactly as written, with no changes to the measurements. Be sure to measure accurately.

Store this jam in a cool, dark place with little temperature fluctuation for 3 to 4 months. Alternatively, for greater assurance of freshness, store it in the refrigerator.

JALAPEÑO JAM

I LOVE PEPPER JELLY, a Southern staple frequently paired with cream cheese and crackers, but I'd never made it myself. Every time I saw a jar, I'd buy or trade for it, but every recipe I'd ever seen used pectin. My gustatory feelings about pectin aside, I'm just not very good at using it — often I can't get the right set, even when I follow instructions to a tee. (Maybe pectin is punishing me?) Finally, though, a client asked whether I could make some pepper jam, so I started experimenting with natural pectin boosters. First, I threw in a few apples, and then I saw a very old recipe in a vintage Time Life preserving book that used quartered lemons. Bingo! The result isn't quite the same as the pepper jellies you might know — it's a little looser, a little chunkier — but it's absolutely incredible with cream cheese and crackers. And biscuits, too!

MAKES ABOUT FOUR JARS (8 OZ/250 ML EACH)

2	lemons, quartered	2
1.2 lbs	apples (3 to 4 medium), finely chopped	540 g
12 oz	red bell peppers (2 medium), finely chopped	350 g
12 oz	jalapeño peppers (about 12 medium), seeded and finely chopped	350 g
1 tsp	kosher or pickling salt	5 mL
3 cups	granulated sugar	600 g
3 cups	cider vinegar	750 mL

Prepare the jars and lids.

In a large pot, combine the lemons, apples, red peppers, jalapeños, salt, sugar and vinegar. Bring to a boil over medium-high heat. Reduce heat and simmer, stirring often and reducing the heat as necessary, until thick. Remove from heat and fish out the lemons, which will now just be soft pieces of peel; discard lemons.

Ladle jam into the hot jars to within ¼ inch (0.5 cm) of the rim. Remove any air bubbles and wipe rims. Place the lids on the jars and screw the bands on until fingertip-tight. Process in a boiling water canner for 10 minutes.

TIPS

I find it easiest to use a food processor to chop the apples, red peppers and jalapeños — just make sure not to chop them too finely!

I highly recommend you wear plastic gloves to handle the jalapeños; otherwise, you'll be sorry.

FOR THE FRIDGE

❧

FOR THE FRIDGE

To safely preserve food in a boiling water canner, it must be a high-acid food with a pH of 4.6 or lower. Foods like soups, vegetables in water and meat or fish need to be canned in a pressure canner, and I don't own one. Yet there are so many delicious things that aren't high acid to put in jars. Well, sometimes you just need to store things in the fridge — we do live in an age where that's not really an issue, after all. Plus, these recipes are all so good the jars won't be taking up room in there for very long.

ARIANE'S MARINATED MUSHROOMS

MY WONDERFUL FORMER ASSISTANT, Ariane Maurice, offered this recipe for marinated mushrooms. I modified it with Indian spices to accompany a lentil curry, and they offset the heat beautifully with their cooling sourness. The beauty of these mushrooms is that they can be made to accompany almost any meal if you change the spices, and they are sure to always be delicious.

MAKES ABOUT 2½ CUPS (625 ML)

1 lb	button mushrooms, quartered	450 g
2	cloves garlic, smashed	2
1	shallot, minced	1
1	chile de árbol, crushed	1
1 tsp	salt	5 mL
¾ cup	grapeseed oil	175 mL
¼ cup	cider vinegar	60 mL
1 tsp	fenugreek seeds	5 mL
1 tsp	brown mustard seeds	5 mL
½ tsp	coriander seeds	2 mL
½ tsp	cumin seeds	2 mL
Pinch	asafetida (optional)	Pinch

In a medium bowl, combine the mushrooms, garlic, shallot, chile, salt, oil and vinegar.

In a dry skillet, toast the fenugreek, mustard seeds, coriander seeds, cumin seeds and asafetida (if using) over medium heat for 2 to 3 minutes or until very fragrant.

Add the toasted spices to the mushroom mixture and combine. Let stand for a few hours before eating or packing into a jar. They will last up to 3 days in the refrigerator, but it's unlikely they'll make it that long, as they are highly addictive.

> **TIP**
> If you cannot find a chile de árbol, you can use any dried red chile pepper in its place.

MRS. CARDOSO'S GREEN TOMATOES

THIS RECIPE COMES COURTESY OF MY FRIEND Bartek Komorowski. Well, actually, courtesy of his Portuguese landlady. He details his love of these tomatoes on his cooking propaganda blog, but suffice it to say that they are *good*. Bartek ate the first jar he received in a single day. Clearly he needed to get the recipe, and I am lucky that he shared it with me.

This recipe must be made with under-ripe, hard tomatoes. Ripe tomatoes will lack crunch and will probably turn to mush when you toss them with the other ingredients. Beware of tomato varieties that are green when ripe! The best option is run-of-the-mill, round field tomatoes.

	MAKES ONE JAR (1 QUART/1 L)	
2.2 lbs	green tomatoes	1 kg
⅓ cup	pickling salt or coarse sea salt	75 mL
5	sprigs fresh oregano	5
5	sprigs fresh thyme	5
5	sprigs fresh rosemary	5
2 to 3	sprigs fresh flat-leaf (Italian) parsley	2 to 3
	A handful each of fresh basil and mint leaves	
2 to 4	cloves garlic	2 to 4
1 to 2	red Italian chile peppers (or a similar variety)	1 to 2
2 tsp	fennel seeds (optional)	10 mL
½ cup	white vinegar or white wine vinegar	125 mL
¼ cup	olive oil	60 mL

Cut the tomatoes into slices about ¼-inch (0.5 cm) thick, placing them in a large stainless steel bowl and sprinkling them with salt as you go. The idea is to sprinkle some salt over each slice. Cover with a clean tea towel and let stand for 24 hours.

Drain off the fluid that has leached out of the tomatoes, either by holding them down in the bowl with a lid or a large plate, or by transferring them to another bowl with a slotted spoon.

Strip the oregano, thyme and rosemary leaves off their stems and discard the stems. (Leave the parsley leaves on the stems.) Very finely chop the oregano, thyme, rosemary, parsley, basil, mint, garlic and chiles.

Add the chopped herbs, garlic, chiles, fennel seeds (if using), vinegar and oil to the drained tomatoes, tossing to coat.

The tomatoes are now ready to eat. Whatever you don't eat right away, you must pack tightly into a jar and store in the fridge, where they will keep for months.

BARTEK'S SERVING SUGGESTIONS

You can enjoy these as a side dish or as a condiment. In the latter role, they are versatile: they go well in sandwiches with cheeses, meats or both! I love to add them to grilled pork chops with cheese. Marinate a pork chop, then fry it in butter and olive oil or grill it. After you've cooked one side, turn it over and cover it with slices of sharp cheese (aged Cheddar and/or Gruyère work well) and a few slices of marinated green tomato. Be sure to let the cheese melt and mingle with the meat of the tomatoes. As with all meats, when the pork chop is cooked, remove it from the pan or grill and let it rest a few minutes before digging in. This allows the boiling juices inside the meat to settle. Enjoy!

CAJUN PICKLED EGGS

MOST PEOPLE DON'T FEEL AMBIVALENT about pickled eggs. They either love them or think they're absolutely vile. Usually, the latter person has never even tried one. But I understand — that used to be me. I'd only ever known the big dusty jars of pickled eggs sitting out at room temperature at weird old bars. They reminded me of medical specimens, not food.

Turns out my graphic designer, Marc, is crazy for pickled eggs. I trust the guy and realized there might be some aspect I'd overlooked. Fact is, they're delicious. Of course they are — they're pickled. My favorite way to serve them is deviled: halve them, remove the yolks, mix the yolks with mayonnaise and pipe back into the whites. Trust me. They're amazing scotched, too; it just takes a little more work (see page 166).

I made this Cajun version to imitate some Creole pickled eggs Marc brought back once from New Orleans — and the entirety of which he ate in one sitting! Indeed, these are quite addictive. Open up a jar while having a beer with friends, and you might see the bottom of the jar before you know it.

MAKES ONE JAR (1 QUART/1 L)

12 to 15	large eggs, hard-cooked and peeled	12 to 15
1 tbsp	Cajun seasoning	15 mL
1 cup + 2 tbsp	hot pepper sauce (such as Frank's Red Hot)	280 mL
6 tbsp	white vinegar	90 mL

Pack the eggs into the jar, then top with the Cajun seasoning.

In a small saucepan, combine the hot pepper sauce and vinegar. Bring to a boil over high heat, stirring. Pour over the eggs.

Seal the jar, let cool, then refrigerate for up to 3 months. They are better after at least 1 week, if you can wait that long.

SZECHUAN PICKLED EGGS

ENJOY THESE EGGS WITH BEERS or deviled and garnished with chili paste and green onion. Try them in Scotch Pickled Eggs (page 166), but spice the meat with five-spice powder and bread them with panko!

MAKES ONE JAR (1 QUART/1 L)		
12	large eggs, hard-cooked and peeled	12
2	cloves garlic, thinly sliced	2
1	whole star anise	1
1 tsp	Szechuan peppercorns	5 mL
1 tbsp	hot pepper flakes	15 mL
1 tbsp	granulated sugar	15 mL
1½ tsp	kosher or pickling salt	7 mL
1 cup + 2 tbsp	black vinegar	280 mL
6 tbsp	water	90 mL

Pack the eggs into the jar, then top with the garlic, star anise, Szechuan peppercorns and hot pepper flakes.

In a small saucepan, combine the sugar, salt, vinegar and water. Bring to a boil over high heat, stirring to dissolve the sugar and salt. Pour over the eggs.

Seal the jar, let cool, then refrigerate for up to 3 months. Like the Cajun Pickled Eggs, they are better after at least a week of marinating.

TIPS

Szechuan peppercorns have an addictive flavor and a unique mouth-numbing quality. You can find them in spice stores or Asian grocery stores.

Look for black vinegar (also known as Zhenjiang vinegar) in well-stocked supermarkets or Asian grocery stores.

KIKI'S FRESH PICKLES

I COULD NEVER LEAVE THESE out of the book, as they are my dear friend Kinneret's absolute favorite thing that I make. Fine, they're fridge pickles, but they are absolutely worth making. They have a fresher, tangier flavor than classic dill pickles, and, best of all, they're ready after a single night in the fridge. Feel free to omit the chiles if you don't like it hot.

	MAKES ONE 2-QUART (2 L) JAR OR TWO 1-QUART (1 L) JARS	
2.2 lbs	Kirby cucumbers (24 to 30 medium)	1 kg
4	cloves garlic	4
4	dill heads (or a handful of fresh dill and 1 tsp/5 mL dill seeds)	4
2	red or green chile peppers, split lengthwise	2
1 to 2	bay leaves (fresh, if possible)	1 to 2
1 tsp	whole black peppercorns	5 mL
2 tsp	mustard seeds	10 mL
3 tbsp	kosher or pickling salt	45 mL
1 tbsp	granulated sugar	15 mL
2¾ cups	water	675 mL
2 cups	white vinegar	500 mL

Cut off the ends of the cucumbers, then cut the cucumbers into chunks or wedges. Pack them into the jar(s), along with the garlic, dill, chiles, bay leaves, peppercorns and mustard seeds.

In a medium saucepan, combine the salt, sugar, water and vinegar. Bring to a boil over high heat, stirring to dissolve the salt and sugar. Pour over the cucumbers.

Let cool, then seal the jar(s) and refrigerate overnight before eating. The pickles should last at least a week if you don't eat them all in the first day or two.

ISAAC'S BREAKFAST BACON JAM

MY FRIEND ISAAC AND I DEVELOPED this recipe in an attempt to make a buck off the bacon craze. Instead of making money, we ended up just having a really good time. It took a few tries, but we felt we hit the nail on the head with this version. It's delicious on burgers, in grilled cheese sandwiches and especially as a garnish for deviled pickled eggs (see page 146).

MAKES ABOUT NINE JARS (4 OZ/125 ML EACH)

- Food processor

2 lbs	smoky bacon strips	900 g
4	medium onions (about 1.8 lbs/800 g), sliced	4
1	apple (about 5½ oz/160 g), sliced	1
¼ cup	packed brown sugar	55 g
½ tsp	salt	2 mL
½ tsp	freshly ground black pepper	2 mL
½ tsp	smoked paprika (hot or sweet)	2 mL
½ tsp	chipotle chile powder	2 mL
Pinch	ground nutmeg	Pinch
½ cup	pure maple syrup	125 mL
¾ cup	brewed coffee	175 mL
¾ cup	bourbon	175 mL
½ cup	cider vinegar	125 mL

Using two skillets, each on medium heat, in batches as necessary to avoid crowding, fry the bacon to a medium crisp, then transfer it to plates lined with paper towels. Drain off all but about 1½ tbsp (22 mL) fat from each of the pans.

Caramelize the onions in one pan and the apple in the other, reducing the heat as necessary to gradually achieve a rich brown softness.

When the onions and apple are both ready, combine them in a single pan and add the brown sugar, salt, pepper, paprika, chile powder and nutmeg, stirring well. Stir in the maple syrup and increase the heat to medium. Stir in the coffee and cook until the liquid is reduced to a syrup. Stir in the reserved bacon, bourbon and vinegar; cook until once again syrupy.

Remove from heat and let cool for a few minutes, then transfer to a food processor and pulse until coarsely chopped.

Return the mixture to the pan, and cook over medium heat for a few minutes more, until it is quite decidedly bacon jam.

Store in jars in the refrigerator for up to 3 months.

> **TIP**
> If you cannot find chipotle chile powder, add another ½ tsp (2 mL) smoked paprika.

DAD'S "PICKLED" SHRIMP

EVERY TIME I VISIT MY PARENTS, I ask my father to make these addictive marinated shrimp. He's never one to use recipes, or to write down what he has put into any given dish, but I did manage to extract this recipe from him. On my handwritten copy (I took dictation), I have written, "Into a strange and different sea." Given the context, I presume this is from the shrimp's perspective.

....

MAKES ABOUT 2 CUPS (500 ML)		
1 lb	medium shell-on shrimp (thawed if frozen)	450 g
	Salt	
1	clove garlic, minced	1
1 tbsp	dried oregano (preferably Mexican)	15 mL
Pinch	freshly ground black pepper	Pinch
2 tbsp	hot pepper sauce (preferably Louisiana or Texas Pete)	30 mL
1 tbsp	olive oil	15 mL
	Juice of 1 lemon	

Fill a large pot with water and salt it heavily — my father says it should be "as salty as the briny sea." Bring to a boil over high heat. Add shrimp and cook until firm and opaque, about 1 minute.

Using a slotted spoon, transfer shrimp to a bowl, along with 3 tbsp (45 mL) of the cooking water. Stir in 1 tsp (5 mL) salt, garlic, oregano, black pepper, hot pepper sauce, oil and lemon juice. Cover and refrigerate overnight or for up to 3 days, stirring occasionally. The shrimp are now ready to peel and eat.

CANDIED PEEL

IF YOU LIKE MARMALADE, you probably like candied peel, too. I always have some on hand — it keeps for ages in the fridge — for chopping and mixing into jams, ice cream, cookies, cakes, you name it. You can also dry pieces of candied peel on a rack, then either roll them in sugar or dip them in tempered chocolate, and they become a candy in their own right.

You can use any citrus fruit except limes, which will turn leathery. Use all one kind or a combination; just keep the total amount to 2.2 lbs (1 kg). You can also perfume the syrup with spices or vanilla. But don't omit the glucose — it prevents the syrup from crystallizing, greatly prolonging the storage life of the candied peels.

MAKES ONE JAR (1 QUART/1 L)

2.2 lbs	Seville oranges (about 6)	1 kg
5 cups	granulated sugar	1 kg
1 tbsp	glucose or light corn syrup	15 mL

Cut off both ends of the oranges, then run a paring knife between the flesh and the peel, removing large chunks of peel. If you wish, cut the chunks into strips. I prefer to candy larger chunks and cut them later on, if I wish.

Place the peels in a pot and cover with cold water. Bring to a boil over high heat, then drain. Repeat two more times. Set peels aside.

In the same pot, combine the sugar, 4 cups (1 L) water and glucose. Bring to a boil over high heat, stirring to dissolve the sugar. Add the peels, immediately reduce the heat and simmer gently, stirring occasionally, until the peels are soft and translucent and the syrup has reduced significantly, about 2 hours. Remove from heat and let cool completely in the pot.

Transfer the cooled peels, in their syrup, to the jar. Store in the fridge, where they will last for months as long as the peels are kept submerged.

CARAMEL CRABAPPLE BUTTER

MY FRIEND CATHERINE LAFRANCE has a company called Dinette Nationale. She makes all manner of delicious things — shortbread, caramels, marshmallows, pâte de fruits — but my most favorite of all is this perfect butter, and she was generous enough to share the recipe with us. Honestly, this is really just the most delicious thing. Delicious enough that it takes hours and you have to make two separate preparations, but you just don't mind. The sour, fragrant crabapples are the perfect foil to the caramel. Slather it on popovers or between the layers of a spice cake, or eat it straight out of the jar, like I do.

The recipe is open-ended so you can make as much as you like based on how many crabapples you have. And if you end up with some leftover caramel sauce, well, no one is going to complain.

MAKES AS MANY 8-OZ (250 ML) JARS OF BUTTER AS YOUR HEART DESIRES

◊

MAKES 4 CUPS (1 L) SALTED CARAMEL

- Preheat oven to 250°F (120°C)
- Coarse strainer or food mill
- Roasting pan
- Deep-fry/candy thermometer
- Immersion blender

Crabapples

SALTED CARAMEL

3 cups	heavy or whipping (35%) cream	750 mL
1	vanilla bean, split and scraped	1
2½ cups	granulated sugar	500 g
1¼ tsp	fleur de sel	6 g
1 cup	unsalted butter	225 g

First make a compote with the fragrant crabapples. Place the whole crabapples in a pot and add enough water to cover the bottom of the pot. Bring to a simmer over medium heat. Simmer, stirring occasionally, until the crabapples are very tender.

Press the compote through a strainer or food mill to remove the skins and seeds, then transfer to a roasting pan. Bake in preheated oven, stirring frequently, until reduced to between half and two-thirds its volume. This will take a few hours.

In the meantime, prepare the jars and lids.

Salted Caramel: In a small saucepan, combine the cream and vanilla bean. Warm over medium-low heat.

Meanwhile, caramelize the sugar in a pot. Put enough sugar into the pot to cover the bottom and heat on medium-high. Don't stir it! Just wait for the sugar to caramelize by itself, then stir in a few more tablespoons (45 to 60 mL). Once this has dissolved and caramelized, add some more.

When all the sugar has been added and the caramel is a nice red color, remove the pot from the heat and pour in the hot cream little by little. Watch out — it will spit and sputter! Return the pot to the heat and cook, stirring occasionally, until a thermometer inserted into the mixture reads 223°F (106°C). Stir in the fleur de sel and butter.

Measure the volume of reduced crabapple compote and add an equal amount of hot caramel. Using an immersion blender, mix well to ensure a good emulsion.

Ladle butter into the hot jars to within ¼ inch (0.5 cm) of the rim. Remove any air bubbles and wipe rims. Place the lids on the jars and screw the bands on until fingertip-tight. Let cool, then store in the refrigerator for up to 3 months.

TIP

Store leftover caramel sauce in the fridge, where it will become firm. To get it back to a fluid consistency, just pop it in the microwave for 30-second increments on High, or heat it gently in a saucepan on the stove. Serve it on ice cream or sandwiched between cookies, or just eat it with a spoon.

COOKING WITH PRESERVES

COOKING WITH PRESERVES

If you are really into preserving, you might find at some point that your pantry is overflowing with more jars than you can give away. So it's good to have an arsenal of recipes in which to use those preserves. Jam's not just for toast, nor are pickles meant only to sit quietly garnishing sandwiches. There are all sorts of ways to put your homemade preserves in the spotlight. Being a pastry cook by training, I tend to gravitate toward sweet recipes, but if you prefer savory foods, don't worry: there are some deep-fried and bacon-wrapped recipes in here, too.

NEW OLD-FASHIONED

I LOVE AN OLD-FASHIONED, but I don't often have oranges around the house. With a jar of New Old-Fashioned Oranges on hand, I never have to worry about that. Plus, I think the resulting cocktail is even better than the original. I like to throw in a cocktail cherry, but if all you can find is a grocery store maraschino cherry, it's better not to bother.

MAKES 1 SERVING

3 to 4	dashes orange bitters	3 to 4
1	slice New Old-Fashioned Oranges (page 90)	1
1	cocktail cherry (optional)	1
	Ice cubes	
2 oz	rye whisky	60 mL

In a rocks glass, muddle together the bitters, orange and cherry (if using). Add ice, then rye. Stir and enjoy.

VARIATION
Use bourbon instead of rye if you prefer a sweeter drink.

TIP
Maraschino cherries are bleached and dyed. While I do have a soft spot for them, they don't actually taste anything like cherries. If I'm having a nice cocktail, I prefer to use a high-quality cocktail cherry, such as the candied Amarena cherries from Italy.

GIN TRISTRAM

LIKE THE SHANDIES I REMEMBER from my youth, but way better — and stronger! I find this very refreshing on a summer afternoon.

MAKES 1 SERVING

Into a highball glass filled with ice, pour the Shandy Syrup and gin. Stir well and top up with ale.

	Ice cubes	
¼ cup	Shandy Syrup (page 100)	60 mL
1 oz	gin	30 mL
5 oz	India pale ale	150 mL

DIRTY GIBSON

A GIBSON IS BASICALLY A WET MARTINI, made dirty here with the addition of pickle brine. It's traditionally garnished with a pickled onion, but you'll find that Dilly Green Beans (page 114) are an excellent alternative.

MAKES 1 SERVING

Stir together, with ample ice, the gin, vermouth and brine. Strain into a chilled glass. Garnish with at least two pickled onions, perhaps stabbed with a toothpick or a tiny sword.

	Ice cubes	
2½ oz	gin	75 mL
½ oz	dry vermouth	15 mL
Splash	brine from pickled onions	Splash
	Pickled onions (such as Maple Chile Onions, page 117)	

TIP

For the best results, choose a very good gin and a nice dry vermouth.

DEEP-FRIED PICKLES

THESE ARE AN INCREDIBLY GOOD SNACK. I first had fried pickles in a little restaurant in the French Quarter in New Orleans while I was on tour. We were passing through town and asked a guy in a record shop where to go for dinner. The next thing I knew, I was eating fried pickles and fried chicken at Fiorella's, along with an amazing Bloody Mary. Best stop ever. Since then, I've been looking for deep-fried pickles on menus, and they seem to be popping up more and more. My current favorite version is from a fish taco place in Victoria, British Columbia, which this recipe aims to recreate. If you like, sneak a few hot pickled peppers in with the pickles to keep things interesting.

I like to serve the pickles with my version of green goddess dressing. This recipe makes more dressing than you'll probably need, but it's so good you'll be glad you have leftovers. Try it on boiled new potatoes or poached fish.

MAKES 4 TO 6 SERVINGS

- Food processor
- Deep fryer or pot fitted with a deep-fry thermometer

GREEN GODDESS DRESSING

1	large green onion	1
1	handful each fresh flat-leaf (Italian) parsley, tarragon and dill	1
½	large avocado, peeled and pitted	½
½ cup	sour cream	130 g
½ cup	mayonnaise	110 g
½ cup	buttermilk	125 mL
	Salt and freshly ground black pepper	

DEEP-FRIED PICKLES

	Vegetable oil	
1	large egg	1
1 cup	all-purpose flour	140 g
	Salt	
1 cup	cold ale (approx.)	250 mL
1	jar (1 quart/1 L) Dill Pickles (page 106), drained	1
	Additional all-purpose flour	

Dressing: In the food processor, finely chop the green onion and fresh herbs. Add the avocado, sour cream, mayonnaise and buttermilk; purée until smooth. Transfer to a bowl and season to taste with salt and pepper. Cover and refrigerate for up to 2 days.

Pickles: Fill the deep fryer with 3 to 4 inches (7.5 to 10 cm) of oil, or according to the manufacturer's directions, and preheat to 375°F (190°C).

In a medium bowl, beat the egg. Whisk in the flour, a pinch of salt and ale until combined, being careful not to overmix (a few lumps is no big deal). You may need to add a bit more ale if you find the batter coats the pickles too thickly.

Cut the pickles lengthwise into slices about ¼ inch (0.5 cm) thick. Place some flour in a shallow bowl and lightly coat the pickles on both sides. Dip the pickles in batter, coating evenly. Discard any excess flour and batter.

Working in batches so as not to overcrowd the oil, lower the coated pickles into the oil in the deep fryer. Fry until the coating is a deep golden brown. Transfer pickles to a plate lined with paper towels and sprinkle with salt. Serve immediately with green goddess dressing.

DEVILS ON HORSEBACK

I LOVED THIS SNACK EVEN BEFORE I knew what it was, just because the name is so weird and tough. In fact, the dish — dates or prunes stuffed with chutney, cheese or almonds and wrapped in bacon — has many variations. My version uses Medjool dates stuffed with a smoked almond and the chutney of your choice (my vote goes to Famous Apple Chutney, page 128, or Devil's Chutney, page 130).

MAKES 12 PIECES		

- Preheat oven to 450°F (230°C)
- Cast-iron pan
- 12 toothpicks

12	Medjool dates	12
¼ cup	chutney, divided	60 mL
12	smoked almonds	12
6	slices smoky bacon, cut in half crosswise	6
	Smoked paprika (hot or sweet)	

Using a paring knife, cut a slit in each date. Remove the pits and replace each pit with ½ tsp (2 mL) chutney and a smoked almond. Wrap each date with a half-slice of bacon and secure with a toothpick. Nestle the wrapped dates in the cast-iron pan.

Bake in the preheated oven for 15 to 20 minutes or until the bacon is crispy. Drain off fat. Sprinkle with paprika, then serve in the pan (they look so cozy in there all together).

SCOTCH PICKLED EGGS

SCOTCH EGGS ARE AN ENGLISH PICNIC FOOD of eggs wrapped in sausage meat, breaded and deep-fried. My father, who was born in England and lived there until his teens, used to make these when I was a child. At the time, I harbored a great aversion to boiled eggs (and eggs in general), and would just peel off the fried sausage and leave the egg. I would do no such thing as an adult, but using flavorful pickled eggs in place of plain old boiled does make me more inclined to eat them. That said, you must still use a well-seasoned sausage blend.

MAKES 10 EGGS

- Deep fryer or pot fitted with a deep-fry thermometer

¾ cup	all-purpose flour (approx.)	175 mL
2	large eggs, beaten	2
1 cup	bread crumbs	130 g
10	Cajun Pickled Eggs (page 146)	10
1 lb	sausage (bulk or removed from casings)	450 g
	Vegetable oil	
	Dijonnaise or mayonnaise	
	Malt vinegar	

This works best if you set up a little assembly line. First, place the flour, beaten eggs and bread crumbs each in their own shallow bowl. Finely coat a pickled egg in flour. Break off a golf ball–size piece of sausage and flatten it against your palm. Nestle the egg in the sausage and seal it into a perfectly spherical sausage coat. Coat the sausage-encased egg in the beaten egg, then roll it in bread crumbs. Repeat, coating it with beaten egg and bread crumbs once more, for a double coat (this will prevent the sausage coating from cracking). Repeat the process with the remaining eggs. Discard any excess flour, beaten egg and bread crumbs.

Meanwhile, fill the deep fryer with 3 to 4 inches (7.5 to 10 cm) of oil, or according to the manufacturer's directions, and preheat to 350°F (180°C).

Working in batches, lower the coated eggs into the oil in the deep fryer. Fry, turning once, for 2 to 3 minutes per side or until the coating is a deep golden brown and the sausage layer is cooked through. Transfer to a plate lined with paper towels.

Let cool just to room temperature, then serve with Dijonnaise thinned with a little malt vinegar. You can also refrigerate them and eat them cold, or reheat them slightly in the oven.

MARMGARITA GRAVLAX

I'M EXTREMELY LUCKY to have Frederic Chabot as my customer. He is a Preservation Society member, meaning that each month he gets two limited edition jars of preserves. Since he's a great cook with a surplus of preserves, he's always thinking up fantastic ways to use pickles, jams and marmalades in unlikely recipes. This gravlax (aka cured salmon) is a perfect example.

Gravlax may seem like a difficult undertaking, but it couldn't be easier. It's prepared in three steps. The first 36 hours serves to "candy" the salmon and perfume it with the flavors of Marmgarita marmalade. Next, it is salted for another 36 hours to firm up the flesh. Finally, it gets a 24-hour rest to allow all the flavors to balance out. It takes a long time, but is not at all time-consuming.

In lieu of the usual suspects — pumpernickel, sour cream, dill and vodka — Fred suggests serving this gravlax with tostadas, cucumber-poblano-lime salsa and a shot of tequila. I must agree.

MAKES 1 GRAVLAX FILLET

10 oz	salmon fillet	300 g
2 tbsp	Marmgarita (page 53)	30 mL
2 tsp	coarse salt	10 mL
1 tsp	five-peppercorn mix, crushed	5 mL
	Lime wedges	

Place the salmon, skin side down, in a nonreactive container that fits it snugly, then cover the flesh side completely with a generous layer of Marmgarita. Cover and refrigerate for 36 hours.

Scrape off the surplus Marmgarita and discard. Pat the salmon dry with paper towels.

In a shallow dish, combine the salt and five-peppercorn mix. Coat the flesh side of the salmon evenly in spices. Wrap it tightly with plastic wrap, place in a dish and refrigerate for 36 hours.

Unwrap the salmon and pat it dry. Wrap it with two layers of paper towel, then with plastic wrap and return to a clean dish. Refrigerate for 24 hours.

To serve, cut the gravlax into thin slices and serve with a wedge of lime.

> **TIP**
>
> Store the cured gravlax in the refrigerator for up to 2 days or freeze for up to 3 months.

ONION JAM POUTINE

THE MOMENT I GOT THE IDEA, I knew I had to put a recipe for poutine in the book — it's Quebec's most famous dish! It is usually a satisfying amalgam of fries, gravy and cheese curds, so I know some poutine purists will object to my rendition, but honestly it's one of the best I've ever had. I just combined the cheese and gravy into one — a riff on fondue — then gilded the lily with Onion Beer Jam.

Etienne, this book's photographer, taught me this method for making fries years ago, and now that I've tried it, I'll never go back. It's such a simple method, but it yields the best results! Do use the duck fat if you can: it adds an incredible layer of flavor.

MAKES 4 SERVINGS

FRENCH FRIES

3.1 lbs	potatoes (5 to 6), preferably Yukon gold	1.4 kg
	Grapeseed oil	
1 cup	duck fat (optional)	250 mL
	Salt	

SAUCE

1¼ cups	rich brown veal stock	300 mL
11.5 oz	Oka or other semi-soft washed-rind cheese, shredded	325 g
6 oz	sharp (old) Cheddar cheese, shredded	175 g
1 tbsp	cornstarch	15 mL
1 tbsp	rye whisky (optional)	15 mL
	Freshly ground black pepper	
¾ to 1	jar (8 oz/250 mL) Onion Beer Jam (page 137)	¾ to 1

> **TIP**
>
> Look for rich brown veal stock at butcher shops and gourmet stores.

French Fries: Cut potatoes into sticks ½ inch (1 cm) wide. Place them in a colander and rinse well with cold water, then dry thoroughly with a clean, lint-free tea towel or paper towels.

Place the potato sticks in a large pot and pour in grapeseed oil until the potatoes are just covered. If using, plonk the duck fat on top. Cook over medium-high heat, stirring occasionally (and gently!), until the fries are crispy and golden brown, about 30 minutes. Remove from heat and, using a slotted spoon, transfer the fries to a baking sheet lined with paper towels. Season with salt.

Sauce: Meanwhile, when the fries are starting to look golden, bring the stock to a boil over medium heat. In the meantime, toss together the Oka, Cheddar and cornstarch. When the stock boils, whisk in the cheese, little by little, until thoroughly melted and blended. Stir in the whisky (if using) and season with pepper. Keep warm.

Put a handful of fries in the bottom of each of four bowls. Add a ladleful of sauce, then a generous tablespoon of jam. Add another handful of fries, using them up, then repeat with sauce and jam. Serve immediately!

POPOVERS WITH HONEY BUTTER

FOR SUCH AN IMPRESSIVE-LOOKING BREAKFAST ITEM, popovers are very easy to make. Related to Yorkshire pudding, these eggy breads rise incredibly high. Torn apart, they release a puff of steam to reveal a perfect hollow base for jam and honey butter.

These work best when baked in a popover pan, which is kind of a deep and narrow muffin pan, but you can also bake them in a muffin pan, which, being shallower, will produce a shorter, but still delicious version.

MAKES 6 TO 10 POPOVERS

- Preheat oven to 425°F (220°C)
- Popover pan, 6-cup muffin pan or 12-cup muffin pan

POPOVERS

3	large eggs	3
1½ cups	all-purpose flour	210 g
¾ tsp	salt	3 mL
1½ cups	whole milk	375 mL
	Softened unsalted butter	

HONEY BUTTER

7 tbsp	softened unsalted butter	100 g
2 tbsp	honey	45 g
¼ tsp	fleur de sel	1 mL
	Jam of choice	

Popovers: Put the popover pan in the preheated oven to let it heat up.

In a medium bowl, whisk the eggs. Whisk in the flour, salt and milk, being careful not to overmix — a few lumps are no big deal.

Take the hot pan out of the oven and, using a pastry brush, quickly grease each cup with a good amount of butter. Divide the batter evenly among the cups, filling them two-thirds full. (If you are using a 12-cup muffin pan, grease and fill 8 to 10 of the cups.)

Bake for about 30 minutes or until popovers rise high beyond the confines of the tin and turn a lovely golden brown.

Honey Butter: Meanwhile, in a small bowl, using a spatula, vigorously stir together butter, honey and fleur de sel until well combined and smooth.

Serve popovers immediately with honey butter and jam.

JAM POCKETS

THIS IS MY FAVORITE WAY TO BAKE WITH JAM. These are just butter pastry and jam, so use your favorite flavor. They need to rest in the freezer before they are baked, so you can bake as many as you like at a time. I like to keep a few in the freezer whenever I make a batch, for lazy Sunday mornings.

Glaze them for an extra treat (and to make them resemble store-bought Pop-Tarts). It's fun to make the glaze match or complement your filling — use citrus juice instead of cream, or infuse the cream with herbs or spices.

MAKES 9 PASTRIES

- Stand mixer, fitted with paddle attachment

PASTRIES

2 cups	all-purpose flour	280 g
1 tsp	granulated sugar	5 mL
½ tsp	salt	2 mL
¾ cup + 2 tbsp	cold unsalted butter, cubed	200 g
4 to 6 tbsp	ice water	60 to 90 mL
½ cup	jam of choice, divided (approx.)	125 mL

GLAZE (OPTIONAL)

1 cup	confectioners' (icing) sugar	110 g
3 to 6 tbsp	heavy or whipping (35%) cream	45 to 90 mL
	Sprinkles (optional)	

Pastries: In the bowl of the stand mixer, combine the flour, granulated sugar and salt. Add the butter and mix on low until the mixture is sandy, with some larger chunks of butter (about the size of raisins — if the pieces are too large, just stop the machine and flatten them between your thumb and forefinger). With the mixer running on low, add the ice water. You want just enough that the dough comes together nicely — not too dry or too wet — so add little by little if you are unsure.

Turn the dough out onto a floured countertop and roll out to a rectangle about 24 by 15 inches (60 by 38 cm). Trim the sides so that you have a perfect 22 by 13 inch (55 by 33 cm) rectangle. Cut widthwise into thirds, then lengthwise into sixths, so that you have 18 rectangles. Spoon a scant tablespoon (15 mL) of jam into the center of half the rectangles. Wet the edges a little, then place another rectangle on top of each. Using the tines of a fork, press to seal all the way around, then prick a little pattern into the top to let the steam escape. Arrange the pastries on a baking sheet that will fit in the freezer and freeze them overnight. (For longer storage, place the frozen jam pockets in a plastic freezer bag or an airtight container, using waxed or parchment paper to separate the layers, and freeze for up to 2 months.)

Preheat the oven to 350°F (180°C). Bake the pastries for 20 to 25 minutes or until golden brown. Let cool completely before glazing or serving.

Glaze (if using): Place the confectioners' sugar in a small bowl and whisk in the cream until the glaze has a spreadable consistency. Use a mini offset spatula to spread the glaze on the pastries. Add sprinkles, if desired. Let set for 1 hour before serving.

> ## TIP
> These are best the day they are made, but are still pretty good the next day. Store them in an airtight container.

JAMMY BOSTOCK

I FIRST TRIED BOSTOCK WHILE WORKING for Patrice Demers at Le Chou, where we served it as the dessert of the day. His version is still the best I've had, but mine's pretty darn good, too. Instead of making the pastry too sweet, the jam brings a welcome acidity, cutting through the rich hazelnut.

MAKES 5 PASTRIES

• Food processor

FRANGIPANE

⅔ cup	toasted skinned hazelnuts	75 g
¼ cup	granulated sugar	50 g
¼	vanilla bean, split and seeds scraped out	¼
1 tbsp	all-purpose flour	15 mL
1	large egg	1
3 tbsp	softened unsalted butter	45 g

SYRUP

¼ cup	granulated sugar	50 g
⅓ cup	water	75 mL
1 tbsp	hazelnut liqueur (such as Frangelico)	15 mL
5	1-inch (2.5 cm) thick slices day-old brioche or carré au lait	5
¼ cup	jam of choice (black currant or peach are good choices)	60 mL
	Chopped toasted hazelnuts	

Frangipane: In the food processor, combine the hazelnuts and sugar; grind to a fine meal. Add the vanilla seeds, flour, egg and butter; process until well blended. Transfer to an airtight container and refrigerate until ready to use, for up to 1 day.

Syrup: In a small saucepan, combine the sugar and water. Bring to a boil over high heat, stirring to dissolve the sugar. Remove from heat and let cool slightly, then stir in the liqueur. Cover and let stand until ready to use, for up to 1 day.

Preheat the oven to 350°F (180°C). Line a baking sheet with parchment paper or a silicone baking mat.

From the top crust, cut a slit in each slice of bread, making an ample pocket. Using a teaspoon or a small offset spatula, fill the pockets with jam. Set the filled breads on the prepared baking sheet and, using a pastry brush, brush them generously with syrup. Flip the slices over and brush the other side with syrup. Spread the top side of each slice heartily with frangipane, all the way to the edges. Sprinkle with hazelnuts.

Bake for 20 minutes or until golden brown. Serve warm or at room temperature.

VARIATION

Use a different type of nuts to match your jam — macadamia nuts with Piña Colada Jam (page 34), for instance (and substitute rum for the hazelnut liqueur).

MARMALADE PECAN PIE

THE FIRST TOUR I EVER WENT ON was thrilling, but it was also pretty rough. We spent two months driving across the United States, sleeping on generous people's floors and rationing the small amount of money we had for food. In North Carolina, we stayed with a bandmate's uncle, who made us the best pecan pie I had ever tasted. I can't explain what a treat that was after miles and miles of truck stop food. I made sure I got the recipe.

In the years since then, I've made it my own. This version uses marmalade to balance the richness and sweetness of the traditional filling.

MAKES 8 SERVINGS

• Preheat oven to 350°F (180°C)

½ cup	packed brown sugar	110 g
3	large eggs	3
1 tbsp	all-purpose flour	15 mL
¼ tsp	salt	1 mL
1 cup	marmalade of choice	300 g
¼ cup	bourbon	60 mL
¼ cup	brewed espresso or strong coffee	60 mL
3 tbsp	unsalted butter, melted and cooled	45 g
2 cups	pecan halves, some chopped and some whole	200 g
	Blind-baked 9-inch (23 cm) pie shell (see box, at right)	
	Whipped cream (unsweetened)	

In a large bowl, whisk together the brown sugar and eggs. Whisk in the flour, salt, marmalade, bourbon, espresso and butter. Fold in the pecans. Pour into the pie shell.

Bake in the preheated oven for 40 minutes or until set. Let cool on a wire rack for 1 hour. Serve with whipped cream.

BLIND-BAKING A PIE SHELL
Prepare your favorite dough recipe, then roll it out to line a 9-inch (23 cm) pie plate. Line the pastry with parchment paper and then fill it with pie weights (I use dried beans). Bake at 375°F (190°C) for 20 minutes. Remove from the oven, carefully remove the parchment and pie weights and let cool completely on a wire rack.

PB&J SCONES

THESE SCONES ARE A BREAKFAST TREAT version of the classic sandwich. I like to think they're healthy, because they have a little whole wheat flour. They are best the day they're baked, but in a pinch will do for a breakfast-to-go the day after.

MAKES 8 SCONES

- Preheat oven to 425°F (220°C)
- Baking sheet, lined with parchment paper

1½ cups	all-purpose flour	210 g
½ cup	whole wheat flour	60 g
¼ cup	packed brown sugar	55 g
2 tsp	baking powder	10 mL
1 tsp	baking soda	5 mL
1 tsp	salt	5 mL
⅓ cup	cold unsalted butter	60 g
⅓ cup	natural crunchy peanut butter, chilled	85 g
½ cup	cold buttermilk (approx.)	125 mL
⅓ cup	jam, jelly or fruit butter of choice	75 mL
2 tbsp	unsalted butter, melted	30 g
1½ tbsp	granulated sugar	22 mL

In a large bowl, combine the all-purpose flour, whole wheat flour, brown sugar, baking powder, baking soda and salt. Using your hands, rub in the cold butter and peanut butter (or use a pastry cutter) until the mixture is crumbly, with a few pea-sized pieces of butter scattered throughout. Gently stir in the buttermilk until the dough holds together. Add more buttermilk, a few teaspoons (10 to 15 mL) at a time, if it seems dry.

Divide the dough into two equal pieces. Place one piece on the prepared baking sheet and pat into a 7-inch (18 cm) circle. Spread with jam, leaving a ½-inch (1 cm) border all the way around.

On a clean countertop, pat the other dough half into a 7-inch (18 cm) circle. Carefully place it on top of the jammy dough. Press gently, then use a sharp knife to cut the round into 8 equal wedges, leaving the wedges slightly separated from each other in a nice circle. Brush with melted butter and sprinkle with granulated sugar.

Bake in the preheated oven for 16 to 20 minutes or until the scones are golden brown. Let cool on the pan on a wire rack for 15 minutes before serving.

BROWN BUTTER SANDWICH COOKIES

BROWN BUTTER WAS PERHAPS MY GREATEST DISCOVERY at pastry school. I remember the first time we made it, in second semester. It blew my mind that you could cook butter, all by itself, until it actually smelled and tasted like toffee. Brown butter remains one of my favorite flavors, and these delicate sandwich cookies really showcase it.

I like to use jelly to sandwich the cookies, because it spreads so easily — Susie's Sour Cherry Jelly with Vanilla (page 70) and Sea Buckthorn Jelly (page 68) are particularly good. But if you're making these for Christmas, I recommend using Christmas Clementine Marmalade (page 51).

MAKES 2 DOZEN COOKIES

- Baking sheets, lined with parchment paper or silicone baking mats
- 2½-inch (6 cm) cookie cutter
- Small round or heart-shaped cookie cutter

1 cup	unsalted butter	225 g
½ cup	confectioners' (icing) sugar	100 g
2	large egg yolks	2
1 tsp	vanilla extract	5 mL
1¾ cups	all-purpose flour	245 g
¾ tsp	salt	3 mL
⅓ cup	jelly or jam of choice	75 mL

In a medium pan, melt the butter over medium heat. Cook until the foam subsides and the butter becomes a nutty brown color and smells amazing. Be careful not to burn it, though! Transfer to a large bowl, scraping in all the dark brown flecks of milk solids. Let cool to room temperature.

Add the sugar to the butter, and, using an electric mixer, cream until fluffy and lightened in color. Stir in the egg yolks and vanilla until well blended. Stir in the flour and salt until a homogeneous dough forms.

Roll out dough between two pieces of parchment paper to ¼ inch (0.5 cm) thick. (These cookies are very fragile and will break if too thin.) Place on a baking sheet and refrigerate until firm.

Preheat the oven to 350°F (180°C).

Remove the parchment paper and use the 2½-inch (6 cm) cutter to cut the dough into rounds. Use the small cutter to cut out the center of half the cookies. Reroll the scraps and repeat until no dough remains (you will likely have to chill in between rolling and cutting again). Place cookies on prepared baking sheets.

Bake, one sheet at a time, for 7 to 9 minutes or until the cookies are golden brown around the edges. Let cool completely on pans on a wire rack.

Using a mini offset spatula, spread the underside of each hole-free cookie with jelly, then top with a window cookie.

> **TIP**
> Store the filled cookies in an airtight container at room temperature for up to 2 days.

JAM-SWIRLED CHEESECAKE

SWIRL ANY JAM YOU LIKE into this cheesecake, but I must recommend Pur Cassis (page 26) — the combination of that tart and musky jam is so fantastic with cream cheese. But that's just me. You could even forgo the jam entirely and instead serve the cake topped with Peach Melba (page 86) or Plums in Syrup (page 87). Either way, this cake, with its modern rectangular form and rich cheesecake on a shortbread base, should please you immensely.

MAKES 8 SERVINGS

- Preheat oven to 350°F (180°C)
- 9- by 5-inch (23 by 12.5 cm) metal loaf pan, lined with parchment paper

CRUST

1 cup	shortbread cookie crumbs	125 g
2 tbsp	granulated sugar	30 mL
Pinch	salt	Pinch
¼ cup	unsalted butter, melted	60 g

FILLING

⅔ cup	granulated sugar	130 g
2	packages (each 8 oz/250 g) cream cheese, softened	2
	Seeds from ½ vanilla bean	
2	large eggs	2
½ cup	sour cream	130 g
⅓ cup	jam of choice	95 g

Crust: In a small bowl, combine the shortbread crumbs, sugar and salt. Stir in butter until well blended. Press into the bottom of the prepared pan. Bake in preheated oven for 10 minutes or until golden brown and set. Let cool.

Reduce the oven temperature to 300°F (150°C).

Filling: In a large bowl, using an electric mixer, beat the sugar, cream cheese and vanilla seeds until smooth. Add the eggs, one at a time, beating well after each addition. Stir in the sour cream. Pour the batter over the cooled crust. Dollop jam all over the surface, then use a knife to swirl it through the batter, creating a marble effect.

Bake for 60 to 70 minutes or until the cake begins to brown around the edges and jiggles just slightly when the pan is shaken. Let cool completely in pan on a wire rack. Cover with plastic wrap and refrigerate overnight before slicing and serving.

FRUITCAKE IN A JAR

FRUITCAKE HAS A BAD RAP, and I can understand why. I was in elementary school when my father showed me the list of ingredients on a cheap fruitcake at the grocery store. I was shocked to see it contained candied turnips! Luckily, my family has always made wonderful fruitcake. This is my version, full of dried fruit and nuts, aged with rum and with marmalade subbed in for the candied peel — not only is it easier, but it's extra-luscious. The cakes are little, and are baked and presented in mason jars, so they're easy to gift. They're so rich that one cake can easily be split between four people. The recipe is easy to halve or double, depending on how many people you intend to spoil.

Feel free to make the recipe your own! Change up the fruits and nuts to your taste — just keep the same amounts. It also works well with a gluten-free flour substitute. You can even leave out the eggs, if you like: this is a riff on a *Joy of Cooking* recipe, and I had the version where a misprint left out the eggs, so that was how I made it for years!

MAKES 12 SERVINGS

- 12 wide-mouth jars (8 oz/250 mL each)

5 oz	chopped prunes	140 g
3 oz	chopped candied pineapple	90 g
2½ oz	raisins	75 g
2½ oz	currants	75 g
2½ oz	dried cranberries	70 g
1	jar (8 oz/250 mL) marmalade (preferably Classic Seville Orange Marmalade, page 48)	1
¼ cup	rum	60 mL
½ cup	Brazil nuts	80 g
½ cup	pecan halves	50 g
1½ cups	all-purpose flour	210 g
1 tsp	ground cinnamon	5 mL
½ tsp	ground cloves	2 mL
½ tsp	freshly grated nutmeg (see tip, opposite)	2 mL
½ tsp	baking powder	2 mL
¼ tsp	baking soda	1 mL
¼ tsp	salt	1 mL
1 cup	packed dark brown sugar	220 g
½ cup	unsalted butter, softened	115 g
2	large eggs, at room temperature	2
¼ cup	light (fancy) molasses	60 mL
	Additional rum	

In a large bowl, combine the prunes, pineapple, raisins, currants, cranberries, marmalade and rum. Cover and let macerate overnight.

The next day, preheat the oven to 325°F (160°C). Spread the Brazil nuts and pecans on a baking sheet and bake until lightly toasted and fragrant. Transfer to a plate and let cool, then coarsely chop.

Increase the oven temperature to 350°F (180°C). Spray the jars with nonstick baking spray (or butter and flour them well).

In a medium bowl, whisk together the flour, cinnamon, cloves, nutmeg, baking powder, baking soda and salt.

In a large bowl, using an electric mixer, cream the brown sugar and butter until light and fluffy. Add the eggs, one at a time, then the molasses, beating until well blended. Gradually beat in the flour mixture, taking care not to overmix. Stir in the macerated fruits and the nuts.

Divide the batter evenly among the prepared jars, filling them slightly more than halfway. Place the jars on a baking sheet.

Bake for about 30 minutes or until a tester inserted in the center comes out clean. Let cool completely, then remove from the jars.

The cakes can be eaten right away, but they are much better when aged for at least 1 month. Wrap each cake in a double layer of cheesecloth soaked in rum, then store in an airtight container — either the same jars they were baked in (washed and with the lids), or in a heavy-duty sealable bag or airtight container. For the first month, douse the cakes with a little rum every week; after that, every few weeks or when you think of it. They will keep for up to 1 year.

TIPS

If you don't have a kitchen scale, you'll need ½ cup (125 mL) each of chopped prunes, chopped candied pineapple, raisins, currants and dried cranberries for this recipe.

I find ground nutmeg overpowering and cloying. Freshly grated nutmeg has a much nicer warm spice flavor. Use a rasp grater, such as a Microplane, or the nubby side of a box grater to grate the nutmeg.

SEVILLE ORANGE MARSHMALLOWS

I LOVE MAKING MARSHMALLOWS — they're a perfect blank slate. This marmalade version is great on its own as a *mignardise*, but would be equally delicious in a s'more. You can even use them to make fancy Rice Krispie treats. A word of caution: avoid making them in very humid weather!

MAKES 54 MARSHMALLOWS

- Candy thermometer
- Stand mixer
- 13- by 9-inch (33 by 23 cm) baking pan, lined with parchment paper or plastic wrap and well oiled

15	sheets gelatin (see tip, opposite)	15
	Cold water	
2 cups	granulated sugar	400 g
½ cup	freshly squeezed Seville orange juice	125 mL
½ cup	light (white) corn syrup or glucose	125 mL
2	large egg whites	2
¼ tsp	salt	1 mL
¼ cup	Classic Seville Orange Marmalade (page 48), finely chopped	60 mL

COATING

⅓ cup	confectioners' (icing) sugar	35 g
⅓ cup	cornstarch	35 g

Rehydrate the gelatin sheets in cold water.

Meanwhile, in a heavy saucepan, combine the sugar, orange juice and corn syrup. Cook over medium-high heat, without stirring, until the candy thermometer reads 240°F (115°C).

In the meantime, in the stand mixer, begin to whip the egg whites and salt on medium-low speed.

Wring excess water out of the gelatin. When the sugar syrup is hot enough, remove from heat and stir in the gelatin.

Increase the mixer speed to medium-high and drizzle the hot syrup into the egg whites in a steady, even stream. Increase to high speed and whip until barely warm and beginning to stiffen. Using a spatula, quickly fold in the marmalade. Pour into the prepared pan, smooth top and let stand for 8 hours or until cooled and firm.

Coating: Sift together the confectioners sugar and cornstarch into a shallow bowl.

If your pan is lined with parchment, lift the marshmallow slab out and cut it on the parchment. If it is lined with plastic wrap, invert the slab onto a cutting board dusted heavily with coating and peel off the plastic. Either way, use an oiled knife to cut the slab into 54 marshmallows. Toss the marshmallows in coating and let stand for 8 hours before packing for storage.

Place marshmallows in a single layer, or with layers separated by parchment paper, in an airtight container. Store at room temperature. Properly cured marshmallows should keep for up to 2 weeks. If they get sticky at all (which the fruit ones, in particular, tend to), just toss them in more coating.

> ### TIP
>
> If you prefer to use powdered gelatin, sprinkle 3 envelopes over ½ cup (125 mL) cold water in a bowl and let stand to soften before stirring it into the hot syrup.

MARMALADE TRUFFLES

IF YOU LIKE THE COMBINATION of orange and chocolate, these truffles are for you. Serve them after dinner, with espresso, and you're laughing. Or make a big batch for Christmas gifts. I like the modern look of a square truffle and, lucky for me, they're a cinch to make that way. If you prefer the more traditional spheres, use your hands to roll the ganache into balls instead.

MAKES 64 TRUFFLES

- 8-inch (20 cm) square baking pan, lined with parchment paper

2¾ cups	coarsely chopped dark chocolate	450 g
1 cup	heavy or whipping (35%) cream	250 mL
⅓ cup	marmalade of choice, finely chopped	75 mL
2 tbsp	orange liqueur	30 mL
½ cup	unsweetened cocoa powder	60 g

Place the chocolate in a medium heatproof bowl.

In a small saucepan, bring the cream to a boil over medium-high heat. Immediately pour it over the chocolate. Wait 1 minute, then, using a spatula, stir in concentric circles, beginning at the center and gradually moving outward, until all of the chocolate is melted and the cream is fully incorporated. Stir in the marmalade and orange liqueur. Pour into the prepared pan and refrigerate until firm.

Lift the chocolate slab from the pan and cut it into 64 squares. Toss the truffles in cocoa. Arrange in an airtight container, separating layers with parchment paper, and store in the fridge for up to 2 weeks or in the freezer for up to 3 months.

THANK YOU . . .

To Eva, the excellent editor of the original French edition of this book,
Les conserves selon Camilla, without whom there might never have been a cookbook.

To my "team," past and present: Marc Rimmer, Liam Brown, Ariane Maurice,
Julie Rondeau — Preservation Society would truly be nothing without you.

To Annie Olivier, Beccah Frasier, Tave Cole, Merida Anderson
and David Lamarche, the generous of heart.

To Stephanie Labelle and Michelle Marek of Cake Club, my pastry soulmates.

To my amazing parents, my preserving aunts and
my (current and former) Montreal family (Ingrid! Tami! Kiki!).

To Kat, for supporting and delighting me, holding my hand and taste-testing recipes.

And, always, to all the Preservation Society customers
and supporters — thank you so much!

INDEX

Library and Archives Canada Cataloguing in Publication

Wynne, Camilla
[Conserves selon Camilla. English]
        Preservation Society home preserves : 100 modern recipes / Camilla Wynne.

Includes index.
Translation of: Les conserves selon Camilla.
ISBN 978-0-7788-0503-8 (pbk.)

1. Canning and preserving. 2. Food—Preservation. 3. Cookbooks
I. Title. II. Title: Conserves selon Camilla. English

TX603.W9613 2015   641.4'2   C2015-900343-1